Bert and I ...
The Book

Also available from Islandport Press
at www.islandportpress.com

CDs

The Best of Bert and I . . .
Bert and I . . . And Other Stories from Down East
Bert and I | More Bert and I
The Return of Bert and I | Bert and I Stem Inflation
Bert and I . . . On Stage: Marshall Dodge Live
Ain't He Some Funny: The Best of John McDonald

Books

A Moose and a Lobster Walk into a Bar
by John McDonald
Down the Road a Piece: A Storyteller's Guide to Maine
by John McDonald
Live Free and Eat Pie!: A Storyteller's Guide to New Hampshire
by Rebecca Rule
Headin' for the Rhubarb!: A New Hampshire Dictionary (well, kinda)
by Rebecca Rule
Not Too Awful Bad: A Storyteller's Guide to Vermont
by Leon Thompson

Facebook

Follow Bert and I on the official Bert and I Facebook page

Bert and I ...
The Book

by Marshall Dodge
and Robert Bryan

ISLANDPORT PRESS • YARMOUTH • MAINE

Islandport Press
PO Box 10
Yarmouth, Maine 04096

www.islandportpress.com
www.facebook.com/islandport

ISBN: 978-1-934031-37-7
Library of Congress Control Number: 2011929921

First Edition Published June 2011
Reprinted July 2014

Book Design by Michelle Lunt / Islandport Press
Cover Design by Karen F. Hoots / Hoots Design
Cover Art and interior illustrations by Nelson C. White
Back cover image by Mark Andres from *Bert and I . . . On Stage*

About Bert and I

"Bert and I come down to the dock about six o'clock in the early morning. Bert went into the boathouse to fetch the pots and the slickers and I went out to the dock to start up the *Bluebird*."

And so begins the first story on the first album that not only launched "Bert and I" as conceived by Marshall Dodge and Bob Bryan, but essentially marked the keystone event of the modern Down East Humor Era.

The iconic "Bert and I" stories were first created by Yale University students Marshall Dodge and Robert Bryan in the late 1950s and performed around campus. The two amateur storytellers soon recorded a short 10-inch album of eleven stories for friends and family, but ultimately pressed just a few hundred. However, growing popularity prompted them in 1958 to record and release the seminal commercial album of New England humor and storytelling—*Bert and I . . . And Other Stories from Down East*. The album depicted Maine fishermen and woodsmen with dry, classic humor and set the tone and the direction of the genre for decades.

Some estimate that "Bert and I" has sold more than one million records in the past fifty years, and nearly everyone who has spent time in Maine knows someone who quotes "Bert and I" or struggles to mimic Dodge's iconic sound effects. Let's not forget that these two popularized the now-ubiquitous "You can't get they-ah from he-ah" and established the dry humor template that would be used again and again across New England.

Dodge and Bryan went on to record three more "Bert and I" albums together and remain the godfathers of Down East humor. The four original albums are: *Bert and I . . . And Other Stories from Down East*, *More Bert and I . . .*, *The Return of Bert and I*, and *Bert and I Stem Inflation*. Marshall Dodge also recorded *Bert and I . . : On Stage*, a live album. *The Best of Bert and I*, a fiftieth anniversary collection of the greatest stories from all the "Bert and I" records, as well as from Marshall Dodge's television show, *A Downeast Smile-in*, was released in 2008.

"Bert and I" are now almost as synonymous with Maine as L.L. Bean and lobsters—they are ingrained in the culture and the lexicon. They may not have invented the genre, but they cleaned it up, popularized it, and pushed it into the mainstream. Nearly every Maine comedian or humorist who has performed in the past five decades owes a debt to Dodge and Bryan. Bert and I. That says it all.

Bert and I

by Rebecca Rule

Bert and I made me laugh as a kid, listening to their stories on vinyl with my country cousins. Marshall Dodge and Bob Bryan's stories sounded like the stories my dad and my uncles and my grandfathers told. In my family, the women tended to busy themselves in the kitchen, while the men told stories, played cards, and—truth be told—enjoyed a nip or two of hard cider. I liked the stories a lot better than the kitchen.

Dodge and Bryan, in bringing Bert and I to life, didn't invent yankee humor—slow, understated, ponderable (sometimes you don't laugh for a minute or two—or until the next day)—but they presented it to the world through their records.

And the world loved it!

Though not Mainers by birth, Dodge and Bryan adopted Maine and the stories they gathered from the fishermen, the clam diggers, the islanders, the hardy Down Easters—those who knew Maine best. The "Bert and I" stories caught the authentic cadences, language, and dialect. They honored the culture of the Maine coast and the New England yankee. They continued a tradition of simple, down-to-earth humor that can be traced back centuries to the Yorkshiremen of England. In this tradition, the listener grins, guffaws, and belly-laughs, but the teller never cracks a smile—never even acknowledges that there might be a little something funny going on in his tale. We call this dry humor. And the very dryness of the delivery makes the quiet punchlines even funnier.

In 2008, celebrating the fiftieth anniversary of the publication of the first "Bert and I" record, storytellers gathered at L.L. Bean (the mothership) in Freeport, Maine, to tell nothing but "Bert and I" stories all afternoon. It was Bob Bryan, Fred Dodge, John McDonald, Kendall Morse, Tim Sample, and me. I was as happy as a pig in . . . a pig pen! To be among those great storytellers was such a privilege. And the crowds (we had to do two shows because so many "Bert and I" fans showed up) were as enthusiastic as they could be. I noticed that as we told the stories, many of the listeners were moving their lips, telling the stories with us under their breath. They knew the stories by heart!

A good story—you take it to heart. And it makes you smile again and again. A good story lives forever.

Did I mention, these stories are some funny? Don't try to read them and drink a glass of juice at the same time or you might find that juice shooting straight out your nose. And that would be painful. Messy, too.

Rebecca Rule has lived in New Hampshire all her life (so far). She is a graduate of the University of New Hampshire and taught writing classes there for a number of years. She is the author of Live Free and Eat Pie! A Storyteller's Guide to New Hampshire *and* Headin' for the Rhubarb! A New Hampshire Dictionary (well, kinda)*, in addition to other books. In the tradition of "Bert and I," she performs regularly in New Hampshire and elsewhere.*

Table of Contents

Stories

About the Storytellers

Discography

Bert and I

Bert and I come down to the dock about six o'clock in the early mornin'. Bert went into the boathouse to fetch the pots and the slickers and I went out on the dock to start up the *Bluebird*.

I stepped into the cockpit to loosen her up with a few turns.

Sa ha ha. Sa ha ha. Sa ha ha.

You could hear it were cold, so I advanced the spark and gave it more choke and cranked her up in earnest.

Sa ha ha. Sa ha ha ha. Sa ha ha ha ha.

Well, I got it started. Bert come out on the dock with the pots and the slickers.

"Throw 'em aboard, Bert."

Bert threw 'em aboard.

"Cast off the bow, Bert."

Bert cast off the bow. He cast off the stern, loosed the springer, hopped aboard, gave the dock a shove with the boat hook, and the *Bluebird* slithered out into harbor.

Bum Bum Bum Bum Bum.

We hit Nun No. 2 about on schedule when I sniffed a cold breeze coming in off the ocean laden with humdiddy.

Sniff. Sniff. Sniff.

That were me, sniffin'.

Woooooo. Wooooo. Whooooo.

That were the breeze.

It weren't long before Old Greasy Frog Light started in a'thumpin'.

Oooo Baaah. Oooo Baaah.

That were Old Greasy Frog.

Presently, we were locked in a dungeon of fog. I couldn't see Bert, and he couldn't see me. I told Bert to cut engine so's we could listen for the *Bangor Packet*, about due through at that time.

"Cut engine, Bert."

Bert cut engine.

"Give a blast of the horn, Bert."

aaaaaaaaggghhhhh. aaaaaaaggggghhhh.

"Give it another one, Bert."

aaaaaaaaggghhhhh. aaaaaaaggggghhhh.

That were a good 'un, but it weren't good enough, for out of the fog, about a hundred yards to port, come the *Bangor Packet* bearing down at a full ten knots.

The *Bangor Packet* smuck the *Bluebird* about midship and drove on through her like green corn goes through the new maid. The water rose up to our necks before we decided to swim for it. I dove down about a fathom or so, so as to avoid the two whirring propellers of the *Bangor Packet* as she went o'er top.

I come up t'other side and cried out, "Bert! Bert, are you there?"

There weren't no answer, so I thrashed about in the water I hit upon a hard object, about a foot or so beneath the surface. Now I grabbed a'hold of it, pulled it up, and it were Bert, only he were full of water. I just held his nose above the waves as best I could, 'til by some stroke of luck we fetched onto a buoy. I clumb atop it, pulled Bert up beside me, emptied him, and we were near dried out by the time a fishing smack come along, picked us up, and brought us back into Kennebunkport, Maine.

Now if you're ever Down East, and want to go a'fishin', you have a standing invitation to ride on the *Bluebird II* with Bert and I.

Camden Pierce Goes to New York

Camden Pierce, who lives out to Mechanics Falls, Maine, was rocking in his parlor one afternoon, listening to the radio set, when the telephone started in a'jangling.

He picked it up; it was the radio station calling.

"Hello—this Camden Pierce?"

He said, "Yes-suh."

"Well, what's the name of that tune we're playin'?"

Camden knew it—"Battle Hymn of the Republic."

They said, "You got it. Besides that, you've just won a two-weeks' trip to New York City."

'Course, Camden had never been out of the state. He'd only been to Bangor once, and that was the time the bull moose wandered into town and was chased into the hardware store by the schoolchildren.

Camden left for New York, and two weeks later he was back. Mayor Johnson had thought it was fittin' to have a reception committee, band and all, and when Camden stepped out onto the platform, the mayor said, "How'd you like New York?"

Camden answered, "There was so much going on at the depot, I didn't get a chance to see the village."

The Sassage

"What's that I smell cooking, Sarah?"

"Why, Charles, that's a sassage."

"What's a sassage?"

"Somethin' new I'm tryin'. Here y'are, see what y'think of it."

"It looks good."

Sniff. Sniff. Sniff.

"Smells good."

Chew. Chew. Chew.

"Tastes good. But after you clean it, there's nothing much to it."

Which Way to Millinocket?

I was standing outside Sutherland's IGA store one morning when I heard a flivver approaching down the street toward me.

Putt. Putt. Putt. Sa ha ha ha.

"Which way to Millinocket?"

"Well, you can go west to the next intersection and get on to the turnpike; go north through the tollgate at Augusta, 'til you come to that intersection . . .Well, no . . . you can keep right on this tar road—it changes to dirt now and again—just keep the river on your left; you'll come to the crossroads and . . . let me see . . . Then again, you can take that scenic coastal route that the tourists use. And after you get to Bucksport . . . well, let me see now . . . Millinocket . . . Come to think of it, you can't get they-ah from he-ah."

The Long Hill

"I've been driving up this hill for two hours. Isn't there any end to it, farmer?"

"Oh hell, stranger—there ain't no hill he-ah. You've just lost your two hind wheels."

The Liar

"What do you think of that man out your way? Would you call him an honest man or a liar?"

"Well, I wouldn't go so far as to call him a liar. But I heard tell by them as knows that when he wants his cows to come in from pasture, he's gotta get somebody else to call 'em."

Set 'er Again

My wife asked me if I would care to bring her mother out for a spin of fishing of a Sunday afternoon. Well, I hadn't seen the old girl in over twenty years, and I was some anxious to see just how she was gettin' on, but I was a bit fearful, because that last time I remembered the old girl, she was workin' her way up in tonnage. Well, I don't mind tonnage in a woman—they're shade in the summer and warmth in the winter.

But when they start workin' their way up in tonnage, that is where you get your problems. Because the more they ton, the more they talk.

And so you can imagine how my heart jumped right up into my throat when I saw the car that that old lady was drivin' in. It was all slanted over onto the driver's side, even after she got out of the car.

Well, we had to winch her aboard. We lowered her real easy, we didn't want to stove in the bottom. And we set her down right in the middle because we didn't want to spend the rest of the day going around in circles. And we was no more than five minutes offshore when that old lady started in; you couldn't squeeze a word in edgewise with a shoe horn.

But we figured we knew how we could fix her—slow her down a bit—so we headed for Otter Ledge. Now, Otter Ledge is good fishin' grounds, and it's nice because the tide sets you one way and the swell sets you t'other, and you don't have to anchor to nothin'; you end up at the same place at the end of the day as you started at the beginning. And as you can imagine, it's very choppy.

We put first one rail under and then t'other, and that seemed to make her a little bit more thoughtful, you might say. Well, she got more and more quiet and then she commenced to breathe quite hard.

And she got quite peaked, and a little green, and then she let out a low moan.

And she flopped right over in the bilge.

Well, we figured she knew best, so we kept a'fishin', and as soon as we'd catch a fish, we'd unhook it and slap it right down in the bilge there.

Well, along toward the end of the afternoon, that old lady heaved up over the starboard rail. We had to rush to port in order to remain upright. And at just that moment, a large wave come along and lifted that lady right up out of the boat!

Well, you know them large ladies is all flotation from the waist up. She must've been all ballast from the waist down, 'cause she sunk right out of sight like a stone—just left a little whirlpool in the water where she was. And Willie and me, we must've poked around for her for fully fifteen minutes with the gaffs before we figured we'd done about as much as we could.

We headed for shore, and I can tell ya that my wife was some upset when we told her what had happened. But we tried to calm her down by tellin' her that her mother'd be back up in another ten days.

Bert and I . . .

Well, sure enough, two weeks later it was, we was out haulin' traps; had an awful hard time haulin' one trap. We finally got it up over the rail, and there was that large lady, draped right over the top. And you know there must've been a good twelve dozen lobsters all muckled right onto her.

"Well," says Willie, "what are we gonna do with her?"

I says, "I don't know . . . but what with the poverty of the fishin'," I said, "I think we'd better peg them lobsters and set 'er again!"

The Mad Dog

"Why are you so het up, Tom?"
"Oh, I had to shoot my dog."
"Well, was he mad?"
"Guess he weren't too damn pleased."

Down East Socialism

Eben Robby went down to the Tremont Temple in Boston one Saturday night to hear Norman Thomas speak. Next Monday, he was preaching socialism to Enoch Turner over the back fence.

"You know, Enoch," he was saying, "under socialism, a person shares everything."

"You mean to say, Eben, that if you had two farms, you'd give me one of them?"

"Yup. If I had two farms, Enoch, I'd give you one of them."

"You mean to say, Eben, that if you owned two hayricks, you'd give me one of them?"

"Yup. If I had two hayricks, I'd give you one of them."

"Or, if you had two hogs, Eben . . . would you give me one of them?"

"Darn you, Enoch—you know I got two hogs!"

Down East Religion

We always said that Tom Ryles shoulda been a preacher. Every Sunday he was the first one into church and the last one out. He even had himself a special seat with his name onto it, right up front by the pulpit. When people came in late, Tom would turn 'round in his seat and stare at 'em.

One Sunday, the Reverend Forbes preached an unusually inspiring sermon about how Christ walked upon the waters.

After the service, Tom headed straight for Decker's Pond and ran right into it, clear up to his neck in the water. Some people come by and asked him how the water was.

He replied, "Not bad . . . not bad at all. I took two or three steps before I went down."

Albert's Moose

Albert Tyler was snoozin' on his porch one mornin' when he was rudely awakened by a moose sniffin' around amongst his carrots. Quick as a wink, Albert had his gun off the wall and shot the moose in the hind leg, just to wound him, you know, so he wouldn't get away.

The moose flopped over on his side and Albert dragged him into the barn and bedded him down for the night with some hay and water—after cleaning the moose's wound, of course. In two days' time, Albert painted the barn a bright red with white lettering on the side so everybody could read it: See the moose, ten cents—fifteen cents, special family rate.

In a week's time, Albert's place looked more like a fair than a farm. A fella come through with his family and paid Albert his fifteen cents to see the moose. Albert took one look at the man and one look at his family, and said, "Here's your money, mister. I don't want it. It's worth a good deal more for my moose to see your family than it can be for your family to see my moose."

Virgil Bliss

Virgil Bliss was the dirtiest man in Hancock County.

Why, he was so dirty that in the wintertime, steam would come out from between his sheets like it comes off of a manure pit. One summer, people complained so much about Virgil just being around, the constable brought him in before Judge Dyer.

"Virgil, have you ever combed your hair?"

"Oh, I did once, but it almost killed me."

"How often do you change your shirt?"

"Oh, about once a year. Why? How often do you change yours?"

"Once a day; sometimes twice when it's hot."

"But Judge, how can you call me dirty when you soil 365 shirts to my one?"

Well, that was all the judge needed. His gavel come down and right then and there he sentenced Virgil to a bath. It didn't take Virgil long to get dirty again.

A month later, Virgil was pulling pots in the harbor when a pot pulled him instead. He sank straightaway to the bottom and never did come up.

People say that the dirt just drug him down.

Chester Coombs's Firstborn

Chester Coombs was that handsome fella who married the Everett girl, and she's kinda pretty, I always thought. But when Chester come back from the hospital after viewing his firstborn, he said, "Lester, you can give me a sharp knife and a soft piece of white pine, and I could whittle ya a better-lookin' baby than what I got."

Arnold Bunker Testifies

I was doin' the swearin'-in down at the courthouse last winter when they brought up that old fella to the stand. He'd been witness to the accident out on the Otter Cove Road—summer people speedin' along had run over one of Oscar Glover's cows, same one that had been clawed by a bear two winters ago.

I got the witness up before the judge.

"What's your name?"

"Arnold Bunker."

"How old are ya?"

" 'Bout eighty-five."

"Where d'you live?"

"Bailey Island way."

"You live there all your life?"

"Not yet."

Bert and I...

The Body in the Kelp

We were clammin' along the beach one Sunday when we come upon a body in the kelp. We didn't recognize the face, but thought it might've been Old John who tended the lighthouse on the point.

We went directly out and knocked on John's door.

"You there, John?"

"Damn right I'm here. What can I do for ya?"

"We found a body down in the kelp. Thought it might've been you."

"Wearin' a red shirt?"

"Yes-suh, red shirt."

"Blue trousers?"

"They were blue trousers."

"Rubber boots?"

"Ayuh, rubber boots."

"Was they high or low?"

"They was low boots."

"You sure?"

"Well . . . come to think of it, they were high boots, turned down low."

"Oh, well then . . . t'weren't me."

The Long Fezzle

My wife Clara died five o'clock this morning. It took me half the day to fix a box for her. I ran out of nails twice, bruised my thumb with a hammer, and split three covers before I got the fourth one nailed down tight. I pulled my back lifting Clara to the wagon, and the halter broke as we come out of the barn, so we had to drive into town with Bessie pulling crooked.

Down the last hill, we got out of control, like, and Clara just slid off the back and shot straight through the post office window. I ran into the post office to see that no one was hurt, and found Tut Tuttle, the postman, peering at me through the stamp window.

"Lucky I had the grating down," he said.

"Sure was," I replied.

"Did you pass the preacher and the undertaker on the road?" he asked.

"Comin' or goin'?" I queried.

"Goin'," he replied. "They started for your place about an hour ago."

"Guess I missed 'em," I said.

"Yup, I guess you did," said Tut.

"I tell you, Tut," I said, "my day's been one long fezzle from beginning to end."

Harry Whitfield's Trip

Harry Whitfield's niece, Winona—the one that's married and lives out of state—asked him down to Oyster Bay, New York, for Easter. Harry decided it might be a nice thing to go down. First, he sent to Bangor for a ticket. A week later, it came back stamped Tunk Lake, Maine, to Grand Central Station, New York, and return.

The day he was to leave, it was rainin' hard. Harry put on his oilskin and arrived at the Tunk Lake station a good hour ahead of time. Sure enough, at 8:30 he heard the whistle, the one he usually sets his watch by. When it blows, it's a good indication that the train is leaving Goodwin siding, about four miles up the track.

Six minutes later, Harry climbed aboard. The only other person on the train was Roger Griffin, headin' for Ellsworth for supplies.

The train started pullin' out.

All of a sudden, Harry felt a stream of water on his neck. He looked up and saw that it was leakin' through the roof somethin' awful. Roger suggested they move, so they got up and went to a seat opposite the stove in the middle of the car.

The train stopped and took on water just east of Franklin. Then they hitched up a load of cordwood near Washington Junction. Then about three miles short of Ellsworth, just as Roger and Harry were settlin' back in their seats, there was a sudden jolt. Harry lurched forward against the seat in front. The train shuddered, then stopped.

Harry called down to Ben Twitchell, the conductor, who'd fallen on the floor.

"What we hit?"

"Most prob'ly a moose."

Sure enough, when they got out, there was a cow moose, starin' into the cab of the engine. She had a few scratches on her, but that was all.

"Turn off that whistle!" called Ben to the engineer.

"I can't! She jammed open when we hit the moose! Besides that, we sprung one of the bottle plates, and the front wheel's clean off the tracks."

Well, Ben went up, took care of the whistle with the blunt end of the fire axe.

Thhwaaccckkk.

One of the section men who'd seen the accident got word up to the wrecker and around two p.m., we limped into Ellsworth.

"We coulda got here faster if we'd walked," spat Roger.

Harry then commented, "Soon as I get back, I'm unloading my ten shares of Maine Central."

That evenin', Harry was going through Portland on the Pullman sleeper, and next morning when he woke up, he was at Grand Central depot.

His written instructions read, "Walk through the station. Get a subway train for Times Square, then get out, follow the red lights until you come to another train. Then, hop aboard for Penn Station."

"Confusin', ain't it?" he'd said to Roger the day before as he was going over the instructions.

Roger had said, "Hope you've got your compass, Harry."

Well, Harry walked through the station, noticing that the ground floor alone covered about five acres.

My, that was a big station!

He got onto the subway all right, but it seemed the entire population of the city of New York was already on the train. Well, suh, she started a-jigglin' and a shudderin', and after a while, started to move.

Everything was all right until he got out at Times Square. His instructions just said, "Follow the red lights."

However, Harry noticed that some went east, and others went west. Harry asked a stranger, who said not to worry, and that he was still confused after riding these trains for forty years. The stranger got him on the right train and not long after, Harry was sittin' down on a seat in the Long Island railroad, the last leg of his journey. The conductor was calling out different stops, "Forest Hills, Kew Gardens, and Jamaica, all change . . ."

When Harry handed the conductor a ticket to Oyster Bay, the conductor said something about changing at Jamaica.

Harry said, "Isn't this the train to Oyster Bay?"

The conductor told him it was.

"Well," said Harry, "then I'm not doin' any changin'. I've spent twenty-four hours up and down, here and there, and now I bought a ticket to Oyster Bay and I'm not gettin' off the train until we get there."

A little later, Harry, just a mite reluctant, changed trains at Jamaica.

The conductor was again calling out the stops, "Greenvale, Glen Head, Sea Cliff, Glen Street, Locust Valley and Oyster Bay train, on track number nine . . ."

By the time Harry finally arrived at Oyster Bay, he'd decided to hang onto that Maine Central stock. Kinda weary-like, he clumb down onto the platform. His niece Winona was waiting, and said, "How was the trip, Uncle Harry?"

He answered, "My Lord, Winona, but that was a long poke."

Bert and I . . .

Tin Roof

During the last hurricane, Harvey Beal lost his new tin roof from off the top of his barn, and she fetched up on the side of Schoodic Mountain. When he went to cart it away, it was mangled and twisted. Obie Cleese suggested he send it out to the Ford Motor Company and sell it for scrap. Harvey crated it and shipped it railway express to Detroit, Michigan.

A year passed, and he got a note from Ford, saying, "We don't know what hit your car, mister, but if you can give us the year and the model, we'll work overtime to get it straightened out for you."

President Harding

Harry Burgess and me was cutting wood up on the mountain last winter, and we weren't there for twenty minutes before old Harry dropped in his tracks right there in the snow and commenced a'groanin' somethin' awful, rollin' around and holdin' on to his stomach.

"Harry," I says, "what ails you?"

"Tom, I'm a'dyin', and I want you to go back down the mountain and tell the folks just how it was."

I says, "Harry, I'm askin' you, what ails you?"

He says, "My wife gave me too much hen oil this mornin', and now I've got the collywobbles. Just look at my stomach—it's all swelled up the size of a shaving bowl. Yup, I'm-a done for."

"Lucky you don't have your belt on, Harry," I says. "You stay right there, Harry, and I won't be gone long."

Well, I went up to where there was an old sawmill and I went in to where the kitchen used to be. I found a jar of mustard and an old tumbler and mixed up half water, half mustard, and took it right back down to Harry.

I says, "Harry, there's just one thing I should like you to do for me before you go."

"Tom," he says, "I should be glad to accommodate you."

"Harry, I should like you to take this."

And I poured it right down his throat and it come right back up green, all over the snow. In five minutes, Harry was back chopping wood, just as good as new.

"You know, Harry," I said, "if they'd done that for President Harding, he'd-a been with us yet."

Not Just Yet

A lady, one of them summer visitors, come into Ephraim Fair's and said, "I would like to be shown to the bathing suits by the woman of the store."

"She ain't around."

"Well, then, I think I'll wait for her."

A half hour later she asked, "Where is your wife, Mr. Fair? I think I'll get her myself."

"She's out to the graveyard."

"How long will she be?"

"She's been out there for eight years and I don't imagine she'll be back just yet."

The Lament of Age

Me and my wife, Rhoda, we're gettin' on in years. Last Christmas, she gave me a set of store teeth. Well, suh, I worked them teeth and I worked 'em, but the more I'd work 'em, the more they'd come loose in my head. Why, it was all I could do to keep 'em there. If I'd bought me a sausage grinder and screwed it onto the dining-room table, I'd-a been a durn sight better off.

Of course, I don't feel too good. In fact, I been feelin' just a wee mite tizzicky. I had a touch of the collywobbles last week, a bit of the ague this, the first time since the winter of '39, and on top of it all, the doctor tells me that I'm losin' my mind. Well, if I am, I don't miss it none.

My wife, she hasn't felt none too good lately herself. She's been sufferin' from sciatica for thirty-five years now. For the past twenty of them thirty-five, I've had to wait on her hand and foot. I sure in heck wish she'd get well or somethin'.

A fella just the other day come up and asked me how old I was. I told him ninety-seven.

"What'll you be doin' when you reach a hundred?" he asked.

I told him I guess I'd take up music.

I went into Rockland last spring for supplies and met up with one of them little Salvation Army girls on the street. She come right up to me and asked, "Dear sir, would you kindly give a little somethin' to the Lord?"

"Little girl," I asked her, "how old are you?"

"Nineteen."

"Well, I'm ninety-seven, and I will pass on before you will, won't I?"

"Yes," she said.

"And I will see the Lord before you will, won't I?"

"Yes."

"Well, then, my dear," I said, "I think I shall give it to him myself."

Bert and I . . .

The Iron Lung

The Fickett sisters run the chowder house in the middle of town. Winona works downstairs in the kitchen, making quahog chowder, and Essie does the bookkeeping upstairs in an iron lung.

Tut Tuttle the postmaster comes in every morning to perk Essie up and adjust the lung.

"Everything's set for the day's breathing, Essie."

"It's a goin'—gasp—a bit—gasp—too—gasp—fast, Tut—mind—gasp—turnin' it—gasp—down—gasp—a bit? That's—gasp—better. Thanks—gasp—, Tut."

Then Tut, that old rascal, he usually gets kinda kittenish with her, and gives the lung a good swift kick to get her laughin', and well, last Easter, Tut and her got to jostlin' around like that, and, she ups and agrees to take a ride in the back of his mail truck to see the countryside.

Comin' out of town, Tut went over the top of a hill too fast, and Essie come out the back onto the pavement.

Tut just leaned out of the cab and said, "Steer to the curb, Essie, steer to the curb."

Well, Essie got out of control and just took off down that hill toward the center of town, hell-bent for election. She crashed through a fence, crossed a field, and got right out into the main stem of traffic on Elm Street. After bouncing off a curb, she ran over the minister of the First Congregational Church and made a bus run into the display window of Simon's hardware store.

Officer Moody took after her on his motorcycle, but just as he'd catch up with her, she'd cross over into the other lane and lose him. By the time Essie hit the traffic circle, she'd gotten things more or less under control and come right round it in good style, and straightened out, headed for home. She lined up for the front door of the chowder house and pulled up just short of the back door, as neat as you please.

Winona looked up from the dishes and said, "Well, Essie, I see you made it home."

"Just—gasp—barely,—gasp—Winona," Essie said.

Bert and I . . .

The Punt

Ed Coney had a little grandson, Tim, who used to stay with him every summer up until the last. Sundays, Ed would give the boy his punt to scull around the harbor all by himself.

Last summer, just before he went back to his parents, inland, Tim sculled the punt over a rock on a wave and stove it in. His grandfather cussed him up and down, and told him to go home and never come back.

When his grandfather wrote for him next spring, Tim stayed home and wouldn't come down.

By the middle of the summer, the old fella passed away, and Tim come down with his folks to the funeral. Tim went right up to the coffin, leaned over the edge, and said, "Well, Grandfather, I see you got yourself a new punt."

The Plane Ride

Two weeks ago, Myron Cudmore and his missus went out to the Skowhegan Fair. This year the featured attraction was a joyride in one of them bi-winged airplanes. The sign on the side of the plane said ten dollars for ten minutes.

Myron saw the price and retreated, when a young fella decked out in cap, goggles, and white silk scarf stepped up and said, "I'll make a bargain with you. If you can keep from talkin' or openin' your mouth the ten minutes we're in the air, I'll give you a ride free of charge."

Myron said he'd take a chance. He stepped in with the missus, and in a whisker, they'd cleared the tents, the Ferris wheel, and were headed for the clouds.

The pilot, soon as he'd leveled off, commenced inside and outside loops, barrel rolls, spins, and the falling leaf.

Ten minutes later they were back on the ground, the pilot looking a mite glum.

"Well, I guess you win the free ride, mister. Wasn't there a moment when you felt like shoutin' or sayin' somethin'?"

Myron, a bit proud-like, said, "Well, no—except that one time when you turned upside down and Ma fell out."

Kinda Poorly

Fred Sawyer died back in '37. They had to dig 'im up last year to make way for the state turnpike. There's a law that says that some member of the family has got to be there when they lift him out, and so Fred's two sons, Paul and Sam, drew lots to see which one would go.

Paul won, and when he come back that night, Sam asked him, "You help them with the diggin'?"

"Yup."

"Was it hard work?"

"Sure was."

"Loam or sand?"

"Neither. Clay."

"How was the box?"

"Not much left."

"You look in?"

"Yup."

"How was he?"

"Kinda poorly."

The Return of Virgil

Hattie Hammond, you remember, she was quite a stepper in her time, she got hitched up to Virgil Bliss. Old Virgil was the dirtiest man in Hancock County before the dirt drug him down. And the reason he was so dirty is because he was so lazy.

Well, suh, he and Hattie were quite some team. They lived together for forty years in the Haynes's cottage, down on the cliff. In '37, part of the roof fell in on them and they just moved the bed over to one corner of the house. Virgil used to brag at how deep the snow would get on the floor:

"I recollect it got as deep in here as it did out there, and it were mighty deep out there, I'll tell ya. My woman went out to the well to get some water with a couple of pails. A gust would come along and I'd lose sight of her, but now and then there'd be a lull and I could just barely see her head above a drift. You know there was times I weren't sure she'd make it.

"Old Hattie, she's quite a card. I went into town the other day and bought a double-bitted axe back home to her and carved HB right on the end of the handle. By gorry, she was so happy that she was out choppin' wood with it before breakfast. You know, something a little mite fancy will tickle a woman most to death."

Toward the end, I think old Hattie caught on to Virgil's tricks and soured on him considerable.

"Virgil, you put that whittlin' stick down and look at me."

"What do you want?"

"Do you know what day it is?"

"It's Sunday."

"Well, this is our fortieth wedding anniversary and you ought to be ashamed of yourself for not thinkin' of it."

"Is that so?"

"You know some one of these days, somethin's gonna happen to one of us, Virgil, and then you'll feel different."

"When it does, I'm movin' up to Kittery."

Virgil used to do a little plowin' in the summers. But of course, he didn't mind that too much because the horse did most of the work. He plowed the crookedest furrow I ever did see. He used to say, "I work awful hard, I tell ya. Yes-suh, there's a good many nights when it gets to be nine o'clock 'fore my shirt gets dry enough to go to bed."

Government Fly

The lumber people have been having an awful time in Oxford County with that spruce worm that lays its eggs up at the top of the trees and gobbles up everything in sight. One of them biologists over to the Academy suggested they send up to Washington, D.C., to the Department of Agriculture for some of them insects that feed on the spruce worm.

The Department sent some insects down, and early last spring they released a swarm of 'em. Last week during the hot spell, Waldo Griffin and Spencer Brown were sittin' out in front of the firehouse, sleeves rolled up to the elbows, when an insect landed on Spencer's arm. He raised his right hand and was all set to swat when Waldo remarked, "Better not strike that one, Spencer—it might be one of them government flies."

Bert and I . . .

Harry's Return

Harry Whitfield decided he'd purchase a ticket on one of those twin-motored Northeast Airline flagships for the return trip from Oyster Bay, New York, to Tunk Lake, Maine. On the day he was to leave, his niece, Winona, drove him to New York City in the early morning so's he could take in some of the sights. First off, she took him to visit the Woolworth Building. Then, they inspected the bomb damage to the wall of Morgan's Bank, and then went up to Grant's Tomb. Actually, Harry argues it should be called Grantses' Tomb, as both President and Mrs. Grant are laid to rest inside.

From there they went to the Battery and boarded a ferryboat, bound for the Statue of Liberty on Bedloe's Island. After they sandwiched two or three thousand tourists aboard, the gates closed and the captain gave the horn a honk.

She slid across the harbor, dodging every conceivable kind of vessel, fireboats rehearsing, sand barges, and a Chinese junk. When they arrived at the island, Harry shut his eyes and braced himself as the captain piled into the slip.

The Statue of Liberty was a gift from the French people in 1884, as a token of friendship. Harry was disappointed because the stairway up to the torch was closed for repairs, but he did get a chance to go up into the crown. He waited his turn at the telescope, but just as he got it focused, it conked out on him.

However, he found the harbor was an inspiring sight with the naked eye.

Leaving the Statue of Liberty, Harry took a cab to LaGuardia Airport to weigh in a half-hour before flight time. They weighed his duffel and fined him for six pounds overweight, and Harry saw a man weighing at least 350 pounds step up and go through without a fine.

He started protesting, "That man weighs at least three times what I do, not counting his valise. What these airlines should do is weigh the passenger—the heck with the luggage! I'd like to herd all those fat fellas into the rear of the airplane and see how she'd fly then!"

Harry climbed the stairs, boarded the flagship, and took a seat up front where he could watch the propellers. The engines roared to life.

They put out so much smoke that Harry wondered if they were burning soft coal.

Then it seemed they squatted at the end of the runway for a long enough time to fly halfway to Bangor. When they commenced to take off, Harry had to hold his ears.

They were almost to Boston, Harry figured by dead reckoning, when Gardiner Hancock, the captain, announced they'd have to land in an alternate field because of fog.

Forty-five minutes later, Harry stepped off the plane at Newark Airport, got into a cab, and said, "North Station, please."

Six hours later at North Station with the cab driver standing by, Harry was wiring for more money. He decided to continue the trip home by railway coach, and went into the waiting room to get instructions. Harry boarded the train and bought lunch at 9:30 in the morning on account of the sandwich fella said it was the last time he'd go through the car.

At twelve noon, the sandwich man was still going strong.

"Last call for ice-cold milk, fresh fruit, orange drink, ham and cheese, plain cheese, sliced-chicken sandwich, cashew nuts, Hershey bars, Almond Joys, *Redbook, Seventeen, House and Garden.*"

Harry wanted a jelly sandwich and *The Youth's Companion,* and had to settle for a ham-and-cheese and *House and Garden.*

At Bangor, Harry changed trains and did some more waiting.

The conductor was calling the stops, "Green Lake, Ellsworth, Washington Junction, Franklin, Tunk Lake, Unionville, Cherryfield, Harrington, Columbia Falls, Jonesboro, Whitneyville, Machias, East Machias, Jacksonville, Marion, Dennisville, Ayers Junction, Charlotte, Milltown, and Calais . . ."

Actually, he was very lucky to get a ticket, because the announcer had said the railroads were discontinuing coach and Pullman service and this was the last train through.

Finally, they pulled into Tunk Lake.

Harry stepped off just in time to see Horace Bradley hitching up the passenger waiting shed behind his team of horses. He bought it to house his heifer in when the railroad decided it wasn't worth hauling passengers.

Horace allowed Harry could have the Tunk Lake signboard. Harry tucked it under his arm and headed down the road, kinda sad and deep in thought. He'd seen the railroad built, and it was hard to believe that he was seeing it die.

He pulled out his watch. Four minutes until eight. She was blowing at Goodwin siding, and in a minute, she'd be out of earshot. He could hear the train whistle fading in the distance.

Which Way to East Vassalboro?

My aunt has a summer cottage up on the crossroads at East Vassalboro, Maine. One day last summer, I was out on the porch rockin' and readin' the newspaper when I heard a foreign sports car come up the road toward us and go right on through the west intersection.

Scrreeccchhh. Scrreeeccchhh.

He jammed his brakes on down at the barrens, turned around, and come right on up again.

He turned around way down at the blueberry factory and came straight on up.

This time he stopped right out front.

"Which way to East Vassalboro?"

"Don't you move a goddamn inch."

The Return of Bert and I

Bert and I come down to the dock at eight o'clock in the morning. Bert went into the boathouse to get the solvent and I went on out to start up the *Bluebird II*. I stepped into the cockpit, walked over to the controls, and pressed the starter.

Vrooooom. Vrooooom. Vrooooooom.

That old Toronado engine fired right up with no trouble, all 320 horses of her.

Bert come down on the dock with the chemicals and dropped them aboard, easy.

"Take her out of the harbor, Bert, while I get the oil boom ready."

Vrrrrrooooooom. Vrrrrrroooooooommmm.

As soon as we got out of harbor, we sighted an oil spill ahead.

"Half speed, Bert, while I lower the boom."

We ran slow along the edge of the spill, scooping up the oil as best we could and pumping it into the tanks on deck.

When we rounded Nun No. 2, we saw that the buoy was all crumpled and dripping with oil. The tanker that must've hit her was steaming off into the distance, trailing the oil slick behind.

"Full speed ahead, Bert, and we'll catch her."

In ten minutes we were alongside the *Machias Marou* and could see the gaping hole the buoy had made in her side.

"Give a blast of the horn, Bert, and maybe that fella will heave to."

"No response, Bert. Give him another one."

"He's saying he's not going to slow down for anyone, least of all a lobster boat. There's only one thing left for us to do, Bert. Full speed ahead."

Vrrrrrooooooooom. Craaaassssh.

We drove the *Bluebird II* into the hole in the *Machias Marou* and lodged it there by putting our shoulders to the bulkhead. We kept the oil spill to a dribble all the way to Bayonne. Then, before the captain served us with papers for ramming his tanker, we started up the old Toronado, backed the *Bluebird II* out of the hole, and headed for home.

"Bert," I said, "get out your welding torch. Get out the solvent and the bait. We're going to repair the buoy, catch the rest of that oil slick, and then, maybe if we're lucky, we'll get in a little bit of lobstering."

Directions

"We are going to Portland."

"Go right ahead. I ain't stoppin' ya."

"Where does this road go?"

"Don't go nowhere, mister. Stays right here."

"May I take this road to Portland?"

"Sure, but they got all the roads up to Portland that they need."

"Is this the road to Portland?"

"Yes. But it's about thirty thousand miles the way you're headed, and there's some stretches that are pretty wet wheelin'.

"Well, is it far to town?"

"Well, it seems further than it is, but you'll find out it ain't."

"Why, look over there—I see a sign with an arrow pointing to Portland to the right, and another with an arrow pointing to the left. Does it make any difference which road I take?"

"Not to me it don't."

"Well, can't you give me any directions to Portland?"

"Oh, you're going to Portland—well, why didn't you say that in the first place? Tell you what you do . . . Keep headin' the way you are; drive five miles till you come to a gray school-house on your right. Two miles before you get to it, you take a left. Go until you come to Amy Ross's store. You turn right just before you reach it, and then you jog two lefts in succession. In a quarter of a mile, go left. Then, in one-half mile, you go right. Then, there's a sharp bend to the left. When you come to it, go left. It's when you get to that fork that we're going to have

Bert and I . . . 45

trouble; I can't for the life of me remember which one of them two roads you take. 'Course, by that time, you'll be so damn lost it won't make any difference anyhow."

"You know, there's not much between you and a fool."

"Just the shoulder of the road."

"Look, do you know where the nearest gas station is?"

"No, I don't."

"You don't know much, do you?"

"No. But then again, I ain't lost."

Gagnon, World Champion Moose Caller

"Oui, monsieur, I am Gagnon, world cham-peen moose call-air. Already when I am born, I am cham-peen moose call-air. I let out my first holl-air in that little cabin in the Allagash, and three moose, they walk in through the door. I reach the age of twelve, and the governor of the state of Maine, he ask me to make a moose count for him. He knows I am the only man in the world who can get all the moose in Maine together at one time.

"I climb up Mount Katahdin to the highest peak in the state, and I let out my moose holl-air. As soon as it bounce off Cadillac Mountain and make echo off Mars Hill, everywhere there is a cloud of dust. I have to climb rocks so I don't get stomped to death, but from this perch, I count 342,698 moose, five Alaska caribou, and a dog with Hawaiian license tag. Oui, monsieur, I am Gagnon, world cham-peen moose call-air.

"Last year when I retired, I am asked to New York to show a group of sportsmen how I make my holl-air. I am scared about what will happen, even though I take out moose insurance.

After the dinner, I get up and give my moose call. Well, as soon as it strike Radio City, hit Empire State, and bounce back from World Trade Center, we hear a clatter of hoof in hallway and doors fly open to show first, ugly nose, then mournful eyes, then massive rack, the powerful forequarters, huge hindquarters of eight-foot-tall bull moose pawing the red plush carpet.

These sportsmen, ha! They dive behind tables and chairs, but I let out a little moose whimper and the moose, he walk over into the corner where he stand as quiet as a baby.

"Next morning, I take him with me on the train back to Maine. When I lead the moose into the woods, I see he walk stiff-legged and I could've swear I see sawdust trickle out of one ear.

"Sure enough, two days later, I receive a letter from one of those sportsmen, in which there is a clipping from *The New York Times,* reporting the strange disappearance of the moose from the glass case at the Natural History Museum.

"Oui, monsieur, I am Gagnon, world cham-peen moose call-air."

The Return of Virgil Bliss

"My wife, Hattie, finally got me to stop biting my fingernails."

"How'd she do that, Virgie?"

"Oh, she hid my teeth."

"How did you court Hattie, Virgie?"

"With a lantern."

"A lantern? That's old-fashioned. I never carried a lantern a-
courtin'."

"It don't surprise me none. Just look what you got, pokin'
'round in the dark."

"Virgie, how'd you ever get to marry Hattie, smellin' like a
bait barrel the way you do?"

"I proposed downwind."

"How'd you come to pick Hattie, Virgie? She's awful plain."

"It's true, she ain't no dresser. But most of the girls nowa-
days, their riggin' is worth more than their hulls."

"Hattie has got kind of heavy, ain't she, Virgie?"

"Ayuh, that's true, too, but she's shade in the summer and
warmth in the winter."

"Who's your wife votin' for, Virgie?"

"Well, the same man I'm votin' for."

"Who's that?"

"She ain't decided yet."

"Understand she ain't voted in the presidential elections,
Virgie."

"Ayuh."

"How come?"

"She don't want to give 'em no encouragement."

"Your roof is leakin' bad, Virgie. Why don't you fix it?"

"It's rainin'."

"Well then, fix it when it's not rainin'."

"Well, then it's not leakin'."

"Why don't you take a bath, Virgie? Then people won't have to run round to windward of ya."

"Well, I kinda like to see what they do when the wind is comin' in off the ocean and I'm huggin' the shore."

"Just out of curiosity, Virgie, when was the last time you washed your hands?"

"Well, last year I was cleanin' a carburetor in a pail of gasoline and I dissolved two or three layers of dirt off my hands. And do you know, I come down to a pair of mittens I had been missing for over four winters?"

"Heard you caught a skunk and trained him, Virgie."

"Ayuh."

"Where do you keep him?"

"I tie him under the bed."

"What about the smell?"

"He'll just have to get used to it."

Bert and I . . .

Harry Sleeps at L. L. Bean's

Harry Whitfield was driving home to Maine late one night after a visit with his niece Winona in Oyster Bay, New York, when he decided to look for a place to put in for the night. But at two a.m., all the motels had their lights turned off. Harry spied a sign reading L.L. Bean open twenty-four hours, so he turned to the right towards the Bean's showroom. Now is as good a time as any to buy a fishing license, he thought.

As soon as he entered the showroom, Harry saw a very restful-looking mountain tent in the corner. While the salesman weren't looking, Harry snuck into the tent and zipped up the front. Though the floor was hard, he went to sleep right away.

At four in the morning he was joined by an unsuspecting lady from New Jersey who was trying out the tent. When Harry grunted, she jumped straight up, ripped the tent down the middle, and fled down the stairs with the tent caught in her heels. The salesman, startled by the commotion, ran out and discovered Harry in the torn tent. Harry, in embarrassment, paid for the tent and got back on the road.

He hadn't gone twenty miles before he had pitched that tent on a grassy stretch and settled in for the night. An hour later, he was awakened by the flashing lights of five police cars on the divider of the Maine Turnpike. For lack of bail money, Harry spent the rest of the morning in jail, sleeping. The governor, learning of Harry's plight, commuted his sentence and ordered the sheriff of Hancock County to come up and escort Harry back home to make sure he got into no more trouble.

As soon as the sheriff waved goodbye at Harry's dirt road, Harry fell asleep at the wheel, and the car, gathering momentum, drove through the side of his house and came to rest against the kitchen table.

His wife, Margaret, looked up from shelling peas and said, "Hello, Harry. I see you're just in time for dinner."

The Silent Chain Saw

"I'm telling ya, Charlie, I'm never gonna live up to the terms of the contract with the paper company. I've got twenty-five cord left to cut and only three and a half days."

"That chain saw we sold ya should do the trick."

"You can have your chain saw. I broke my back with the darn thing. The weight of it almost killed me, and I only cut two cords the whole week."

"Well, just a minute—let me start it up."

Waaaaaaaahhhhhh.

"What's that noise?"

M'am Hackett's Compost Heap

I shall never forget that homeward passage back to Castine when I was mate aboard the *Lida B.* I went below to speak to the old man who was in his cabin on his beam end, so to speak, with a cruel rheumatism.

"Captain Philips, we are too close in with the land, the fog is too thick, and the wind too fresh to be carrying so much canvas. May I shorten sail, sir?"

The old man reared up in his bunk, and piercing me with his steel-gray eyes, said, "Sound, and pass the lead below."

I went on deck and heaved the lead myself, for I wished no slip-ups. Returning below, I cried, "Five fathoms with sand, sir, and a cracking good breeze."

"Let me see that lead, Mr. Salter."

And out of the hollow at the base of the lead, he scraped the sand brought up from the bottom. With his right forefinger, he placed a pinch of the sand on his tongue.

"Don't you mean seven fathoms, Mr. Salter?"

"Seven fathoms it was, sir, but I subtracted two to be on the safe side."

"Right, Mr. Salter, right; I am glad to find you so particular. We are close in with the land and cannot be too careful. You must keep this vessel northeast, half east, straight as a gun barrel. Shake out all reefs, Mr. Salter, and we shall bring this schooner home in style. If you do not hear the sound of breakers in just fifteen minutes, let me know it."

Well, in fifteen minutes exactly, I heard the roar of breakers.

"Luff, luff and shake her," I cried.

The *Lida B.* was brought to the wind in an instant, and the dark line of Castine just fifty yards off our stern told us all was well.

After we had anchored, I determined to put the old man to a test, for I could not see how he could navigate so well with nothing more to go on than a pinch of sand. I swung the lead 'round my head like David's sling, and hurled it high on Castine's shore. Then I hauled the lead back aboard and took it below.

"Captain Philips," I said, "the fifteen minutes are gone. It blows spitefully in flaws and spits thick, sir. We still have not heard the sound of breakers."

"Mr. Salter," returned the old man, "northeast, half east should have brought you within earshot of the breakers some minutes ago. I am afraid you have not kept this vessel straight. Now, let me see that lead."

The captain tasted the dirt in the lead and spat it all over the cabin floor.

"There is no fault in your steering, Mr. Salter. You have held this vessel straight as a gun barrel. But I regret to inform you that Castine has sunk and we have sailed directly over M'am Hackett's compost heap."

Bert and I . . .   55

Bert and I and the Bricks

Bert and I tore out Bert's chimney and had to get a pile of chimney bricks off the attic floor and down cellar.

"You know, Bert," I said, "these old bricks are worth a lot of money, so load them into the barrel easy. I guess if we store them down cellar, we'll have to guard the cellar like Fort Knox. Get a rope on that barrel, Bert, and run it through the pulley on the rafter above you, and down to me here in the cellar. Now, ease that barrel to the edge of the attic floor as I pull on the rope from this end."

Well, when we swung that barrel off the attic floor into the air, it appeared it weighed more than I did, 'cause it headed down and I headed up. The barrel met me halfway and took a good deal of me with it. Because I refused to let go, I jammed my fingers in the pulley and bounced my head off the rafter. And when the barrel hit the cellar floor, the bricks come out of the bottom of it, and then it appeared that I weighed more than the barrel, for it headed up and I headed down. I met the barrel halfway again, and what the barrel didn't do to me in the first place, it did to me in the second. I landed on the cellar floor so hard, I let go of the rope, and the barrel come down and hit me on the head. When I come to, I was inside that barrel, settin' on top of the pile of broken bricks.

"Bert," I said, "that should be a lesson to both of us. If you try and hold on to something of value these days, through all the ups and downs, you'll end up in a barrel for sure. All smashed up and nothin' to show for your efforts but a pile of dust."

At the Graveyard

"Sorry to hear that you're burying your pa."

"Got to. He's dead."

"They say he was a self-made man."

"If he was, it sure relieves the Almighty of considerable responsibility."

"You the gravedigger?"

"Ayuh."

"Isn't that grave too shallow?"

"Maybe. But he ain't never gonna get out."

"How come this graveyard has no fence around it?"

"Why put a fence up when them on the inside can't get out, and them on the outside aren't in any hurry to get in?"

"Ever had a family that refused to pay you after you had dug a grave?"

"They pay or up he comes."

"What's the death rate 'round here?"

"About one to a person."

"You been askin' all the questions. Let me ask you one: How old are ya, anyway?"

"Ninety-two."

"Huh . . . hardly pays you to go back to town."

The Captain and the Lady

"Will the fog lift, Captain?"

"Madam, might be it might, and might be it mightn't, but it won't if it ain't a mind to."

"Captain, I see you have a drought here, too, like we have back in New York City."

"No, Madam—it is low tide."

"Captain, I hear you talking to yourself often. Are you lonely?"

"I like to talk to an intelligent man, and I like to hear an intelligent man speak."

"What a terrible mess that seagull has made on your lapel, Captain. I'll be right back with some toilet paper."

"Don't bother, Madam. By the time you find that toilet paper, that seagull will be a mile from here."

"Good heavens. Wasn't that a rock we just struck?"

"Yes it was."

"Didn't you know where that rock was?"

" 'Course I did. Hit it, didn't I?"

"Do you own another boat beside this one, Captain?"

"Ayuh."

"Where is she?"

"On the bottom."

"Do you intend to sail her again?"

"Not where she is."

"Captain, am I right in saying you raise minks on the side?"

"You are correct, Madam."

"How often do you skin them?"

"More than once a year makes them nervous."

"What are those fish doing in that bucket?"

"Saving 'em for my cow."

"Do you feed your cow fish?"

"Ayuh. She thrives on 'em."

"What does her milk taste like after eating fish?"

"Cussed strong of mackerel."

"Do you drink it that way?"

"No. But heat it, and slice an onion into it, and you've got the finest fish chowder in all New England."

"Captain, I understand that you are one of the biggest liars along the coast of Maine."

"I believe that is what my reputation is. And may I say, Madam, that you are one of the most beautiful ladies I have ever seen."

The Chicken Truck

"I'm sorry to pull you over like this, mister. You weren't speeding or nothing like that, but I'm just curious about why you stop every ten miles and hit the side of your truck with a baseball bat."

"It's this way, Officer. I've got a one-ton truck here, and three tons of chickens in the back, and I've got to keep two tons in the air all the while."

Harry Startles Wiscasset

Harry Whitfield bought his wife Margaret a truck camper for their fortieth wedding anniversary 'cause he knew she'd be so tickled pink, she'd do all the driving. When people saw her at the wheel of the truck camper alone, they wondered where Harry was. He was in the back, sleeping.

One time, she started the camper up with a jerk and Harry, who was just stepping into his pajamas, was thrown out the back door onto the main street of Wiscasset. Miss Rhoda Beal, the librarian, who was in the car behind Harry, drove up onto the sidewalk and scooped Charlie Somes, the local game warden, onto her hood. Traffic backed up across the bridge as far as the eye could see. Meanwhile, Margaret was halfway to Bath, none the wiser.

When Harry spied a telephone booth over the heads of the onlookers, he jumped up and made a dash for it. As soon as he closed the door behind him, he realized he was in a glass booth and he'd just turned on the light. Then he saw he was still clutching his pajamas. Just as Harry got 'em on, Sergeant Wormwood drove up and thought Harry was the escaped convict he was looking for.

Next morning, Margaret was at the Thomaston Jail with a large cake.

Harry walked out the gate past Margaret in a huff.

"Next time, Maggie," he said, "let the clutch out slow."

Bert and I Stem Inflation

Bert and I decided to go to Washington to stop the inflation. We took the *Bluebird VI* down channel, out of Kennebunkport and out to sea, heading south.

"Bert," I said, above the roar of the engine, "if we can slow them Treasury presses down, on the ones and fives especially, we'll stop inflation dead."

After a pleasant trip on the Chesapeake, we sailed up the Potomac, moored in the tidal basin, and went straight to the White House to see if the president were there. We snuck in with a group of Norwegian diplomats, and when it come time to shake hands with the president, we got him off to one side and asked him if there might be something he could do about the price of bait. He told us to go to the Cabinet.

"It's halfway down the hall on the left, Bert," I said. "I saw it on the way in."

Darnedest thing—we opened the door to that cabinet, and who should be there, but the top economical advisor, a'talkin' to himself. We just stood there and got a free lecture on the national gross product, the gold preserves, easing up on definite spendin', and bubble-up and trickle-down, whatever that was.

"Bert," I said, as I shut the door to the cabinet, "that economist can talk all he wants about raisin' this and lowerin' that, but if he would just slow the money presses down, particularly on the ones and fives, we would stop inflation cold."

When we finally got over to the presses, we could see they were going flat-out, except for a bottleneck at the desk of a little man in a green visor. He was all shrunk up, except for his huge right arm, which moved like lightning, signing them bills. It was the secretary of the Treasury.

"Mr. Secretary," I shouted above the roar. He looked up, his arm never stopping. "Mr. Secretary—the law says you should sign your full name on every bill, no initials."

He gave me the dirtiest look and the wind went right out of him. He looked like he was gonna cry for a moment, but slowly, he picked up rhythm, and he begun signing his whole name on them bills for the first time. And that was the way Bert and I slowed the presses by a third and brung the economy back to normal.

Bert and I...

No News

"Hello, Virgie. I appreciate your comin' down to the station to meet me after my being away so long. I know it was the doctor's orders not to send me any news of the goings-on at home. But now tell me everything, Virgie. What's the news?"

"Well, sir, there's no news. Except your dog died."

"Oh no, Virgie, not my prize dog! That's terrible! What happened?"

"Well, sir, he ate some of that burnt horse flesh."

"Burnt horse flesh! How did he get that?"

"Well, when the barn burned down—"

"The barn! Oh no! How did that happen?"

"Well, a spark flew from the house."

"The house?!"

"Yes sir, that's all gone. The house caught on fire, the sparks, they flew to the barn, the barn burned down, burned up the horses, the dog ate some of that burnt horse flesh and died."

"Oh, Virgie—how did the house catch on fire?"

"Well, sir, it was the candles that caught onto the curtains."

"The candles! You know I have never allowed candles in the house. What were you doin' with candles?"

"They were all around the coffin."

"The coffin! Who died?"

"Well, that was your mother-in-law."

"Oh well, I am sorry to hear that. Just how did she die?"

"Your mother-in-law died of the shock of your wife runnin' off with the stable boy. And aside from that, there is no news."

The Bear in the Spring

A city slicker come to the Maine woods to rough it. His guide sent him off to the spring to fetch a pail of water. That slicker come back in the cabin in one minute time, all feather-white with fear and the pail empty and rattlin' in his right hand.

"What on earth is the matter with you?" asked the guide.

"There's a bear, and he's standing up to his belt-line in that spring," replied the slicker.

"Well, for heaven's sakes, that bear's just as afraid of you as you are of him."

"Oh," replied the slicker, "well, then, in that case, then that water wouldn't be fitting for to drink anyhow."

The Pet Turkey

When I was a boy, my father gave me a turkey chick to raise and fatten for Christmas dinner. He grew into a fine, fat gobbler, and just before Christmas, my father told me to kill the bird, pluck him, and clean him. Well, I looked at the turkey and he looked at me, and I told my father I'd wait a little bit longer.

Come Christmas Eve, Father told me I'd have to kill the bird or he would. I looked at the bird and he looked at me, and I told Father that I'd take care of it after Father'd gone to bed. I looked at the bird and he looked at me, and I didn't have the heart to kill him, so I fed him whiskey and I plucked him and I put him in the 'frigerator.

Next morning when Father opened up the 'frigerator door, that turkey come out a'struttin' all over the kitchen floor, proud and naked as the day he was born. And you know, we never did kill that bird. My father and me, we spent the rest of Christmas Day knittin' him a sweater.

Bert and I . . .

Too Late, Mr. Perkins

Mr. Perkins come down to my place this mornin' and asked me if I would build him a new privy.

I said, "Mr. Perkins, where was you aimin' for to build it?"

He said, "T'other side of the lot, by the lilacs. And then it'll be real pleasant in the spring."

"Well," I said, "Mr. Perkins, it's your privy."

And I got as far as the floorboards and Mr. Perkins come out and said, "Sy, I've been thinkin' some more about this privy, and if it's t'other side of the lot by the lilacs, it's gonna be awful far in the winter," he said. "If it was over this side of the lot by the chestnuts, it'd be much more convenient them cold winter months."

"Well," I said, "Mr. Perkins, it's your privy."

I got as far as the roofing and Mr. Perkins come out and he said, "Sy, I've been thinkin' some more about this privy of mine, and it seems to me, if it's this side of the lot, by the chestnuts, what with the prevailing wind being sou-sou'west, and the house standing just nor-nor'east of that privy, it's gonna be awful uncomfortable for the lady folks in the kitchen during the summer months. So I think if we had this privy halfway between the lilacs and the chestnuts, then neither would it be too far in the winter nor too close in the summer."

"Well," I said, "Mr. Perkins, it's your privy."

And I got as far as what you might call the interior decoratin' when Mr. Perkins come out, and he was all het up. He said, "Consarn it, Sy, I told you from the very start that I wanted a two-hole privy and there you've gone ahead and framed it up as a one-holer."

"Well," I said, "Mr. Perkins, it's your privy, and I don't want to seem to be dictatin' to you or nothin' like that, but it seemed to me that if I'd framed it up as a two-holer and you'd come out to it some night, should we say, pressed for time, before you made up your mind which one of them two holes to set on, Mr. Perkins, it'd be too late, that's all."

Texas vs. Maine

"I don't know about your farm in Maine, mister, but I have a ranch in Texas that is so large it takes me five days to drive around my entire spread."

"I have a car just like that, myself."

Frost, You Say

"Frost, you say? You ask me if I had any frost to my place this mornin'?

"Why, I'll tell ya, this mornin' I woke up about five o'clock, and I'll say there ain't never been a lay-a-bed in the Bliss family for as long as anyone can remember. Well, I jumped into my pants and pulled on my boots and headed down over them stairs o' mine. Now, them stairs, I don't want no steep, narrow stairs where you break your damn neck goin' down 'em like a ladder. My stairs have got twelve-inch treads and only five-inch risers and you don't hear no hollerin' out of 'em, neither, because they're made out of solid oak, and alongside of them stairs I got me a red cherry banister and at the foot, a newel post made out of curly ash, and the combination of red cherry and curly ash is awful nice in the early-morning light when you come down to do your chores.

"Well, now at the foot of them stairs I got me a nice setting room and at the corner of that setting room, I got me a red plush sofa, and at the head of it, a standing lamp with a circular, cream-colored globe, and I don't think nothin' of lyin' on that sofa until almost eight-thirty, a'readin' *The Clarion* on Thursdays when it comes out before I go to bed.

"Well, after I pass through the setting room I went into the dining room, and I've got wainscotin' all around that dining room made out of butternut wood. I want to tell you, if you've got yourself a dining room, you ought to have the wainscotin', and if you've got wainscotin', you ought to have butternut wood, because it just gives you an appetite to look at it, I want to tell ya.

"Well, then, I went into my kitchen, and in the center of that kitchen, I got me a big, black Clarion stove, and that stove's got five, six controls on it, and it takes more than a teaspoonful of brains to operate, but maybe that's why there ain't so many of them stoves around today. Now, I can cook six or seven dishes on it all at onc't, and have 'em all come out just perfect. Over on the left is a searing area where I sear steaks and try out bacon, and in the center, that's the waiting area, where the pork waits for the beans and the butter waits for the clams. Over on the right, that's a simmerin' area, where I simmer bones for making soup. Up above that stove, I got me some cupboards, metal cupboards built right into the stove, you know, and that's where you're supposed to keep your salt and pepper and cereals to keep them dry; well, that's where I stuff my bills for aging, for a few months.

"And then I burn nothin' but raw rock maple and birch in that stove, because the smoke kind of works its way through the stove lids and through the pots and pans, right through 'em, and

into the food, and gives the food the best flavor you ever did taste. Now, I want to tell ya, yes . . .

"Well, after I got through with the kitchen there, I headed out toward my privy. Now, I always say that a fella who ain't regular in his habits ain't gonna amount to a hill of beans. And if you're gonna be regular, you've got to have a well-built privy. A privy built quarterin' into the wind makes a might side of difference with a draft that comes up through the holes, and you've got to have your privy seats made out of boxwood because they make mighty soft and velvety, and they don't develop no cracks—and them cracks can prove real startling.

"Well, after I got through with my privy there, I headed out to my cow pasture. Now, the Lord giveth and He taketh away, but my cows taketh and give back five-fold, I want to tell ya. I had just opened the gate to let the cows out to pasture, when I happened to look down on the ground, and do you know, there on the grass was just a little, a little mite of frost."

Harry Rawls

"Howdy-do, Mr. Rawls."

"I am not Mr. Rawls."

"You sure you ain't?"

"I don't even know a Mr. Rawls."

"You're the spittin' image of Harry Rawls."

"Just a coincidence, I assure you."

"By Godfrey, you are Harry Rawls, and you don't even know it."

Life Insurance

"How is this man related to you?"

"My father."

"And he was covered under this policy?"

"Ayuh."

"And how did the accident occur?"

"Fell off the barn roof."

"How far did he fall?"

"Forty feet."

"How did he die?"

"Broken neck."

"Thank you very much for your cooperation in what must be trying circumstances. Any remarks?"

"He didn't make none."

Lewis Bayard and the Judge

"Lewis Bayard, you've been arrested twice in a year for drunkenness, and the law says I've got to fine you five dollars."

"Oh, that's all right, Judge. I know you're just doin' your job, but do I get somethin' to show for this?"

"Well, you've got a big head, haven't you?"

"But I mean a piece of paper, to say I've paid my fine."

"Oh, you mean a receipt. We'll give you a receipt. Don't you trust us?"

"Oh, I trust you, Judge, but you and I are gettin' old now, and soon we'll be passin' on and meetin' our Maker. And when I show up at the pearly gates and St. Peter asks if I've ever been drunk, I'll say I have. And he'll ask me if I've ever been arrested, and I'll say I was. And he'll ask me if I ever had to go to court, and I'll say I did. He'll ask me if I was fined, and I'll tell him I was. And he'll say, 'Did you pay your fine?' and Judge, if I don't have that receipt, they'll be huntin' all over hell for Judge Saywood to see if I paid my fine."

Bert and I Solve the Energy Crisis

Bert and I come down to the dock around five in the morning. Bert went into the woodshed for some kindling, and I went down to the dock to start up the *Bluebird III*.

Since the beginning of the fuel crisis, we had torn the old Knox Marine make-and-break one-lunger out of the cockpit, and had installed Bert's black Clarion stove in its place. The hot-water heater on the side of the stove is the boiler; for a piston, Bert's son, Forrest, threw in his bicycle pump; and my Aunt Mehitabel contributed the mill wheel off her cake factory since she had converted to crumb power. I just got the stove goin' when Bert come down on the dock with an armload of wood.

"Throw it aboard, Bert."

Bert threw it aboard.

An hour later, after we got up enough pressure, Bert cast off and the *Bluebird* steamed out into harbor.

Since we didn't have as much power with steam as we had with gas, we cut two feet off the bottom of the hull and added them onto the sides, so we slipped along on top like a riverboat instead of plowing through like a destroyer. We drew so little water we could go through the shallows and make shortcuts.

About when we should've sighted Nun No. 2, a fog set in, thick. Bert had forgotten to compensate the compass since installing the stove, so we thought we could head for Greasy Frog Light for our bearing, but the Coast Guard had slowed the signal down to once every two hours to conserve electricity, and you could go quite far in the wrong direction during the intermission. And even when we got close, we knew we would not be able to see the beam from the fifty-watt bulb they had just installed, so we just kept moving and hoped we'd hit land before long.

We kept a'churnin' all afternoon, and when it got dark we figured the sun must've gone down. Then, there was a terrible crashin', and we hit the steepest seas I had ever felt. I had never been so badly tossed about in all my days, and the strange thing was, there weren't no wind—no wind at all—not a breath of air.

"Keep a'churnin', Bert."

Bert kept a'churnin' through the night.

About four in the mornin', we come up hard on a ledge. *Craaaaaaussssh.*

That was the *Bluebird*, grindin' out on a ledge.

"We'll have to wait here for high tide to float us off, Bert," I said.

But when the sun come out, an hour later, we could see we were perched on a rock, in the middle of someone's back yard all the way up in Days Mills. We had sailed ten miles overland on a heavy autumn dew. The rough seas were really rocks and rills.

We didn't waste no time gawkin'. We borrowed a lawn sprinkler, hitched it to the bilge pump, set it up on the bow, got it sprinklin', got enough water under us, and we slid right off that ledge in good style and headed back toward the sea.

Just as we were crossin' Route 1, it all of a sudden come to us—we were goin' faster on land than we'd ever gone through the water—so we squared away in the right lane, headin' north.

"Better slow down, Bert, we're goin' over the fifty-mile-an-hour limit."

"But we're burnin' wood, not gas," Bert replied.

Just then, we heard a si-reen.

"All right, where are the plates on this contraption?"

"On the paddlewheel, Officer—but it's goin' around too fast for you to see."

When he asked me for my driver's license, I showed him my lobster fisherman's permit. That did it, I guess, and he jumped up into a nearby tree and refused to come down. They say he's up there still . . . trying to conserve energy, I guess.

Buryin'

"You look pretty spruce, Charlie. Where're you goin'?"
"Buryin'."
"Kinda early for strawberries."
"It's my mother-in-law."

The Whole Load

Reverend Forbes had just a single person in his congregation one Sunday—Henry Treat, a farmer of seventy-eight. The hymn sounded reedy with only Henry, the Reverend Forbes, and Miss Twombly, the organist, to sing it. The Psalms didn't do so bad, though, 'cause Henry liked to shout the responses right out. Then the reverend scratched his head, peered over the pulpit, and asked Henry in a whisper if he should go ahead and deliver the sermon with only Henry and Miss Twombly there to hear it.

Henry replied that when only one calf appeared at feeding time, he fed it.

Reverend Forbes delivered a spirited sermon, lasting two hours. After the service, when the reverend shook Henry's hand at the door, Henry confided that while he would go ahead and feed just one calf, he would not feed it the whole load.

Suicide

I lost so much on the stock market, I decided to end it all. So I drove into town and bought a bottle of carbolic acid, a can of gasoline, a length of strong rope, and a big horse pistol. I threw one end of the rope over a branch of the tree that spreads out over the river, and I tied the other end of the rope around my neck. Then I swallowed the carbolic acid, doused myself with the gasoline, and lit it.

I kicked off the bank, swung out over the river, putting that big horse pistol to my head. I fired and missed, severing the rope instead. I plunged into the water, dousing the flames. I swallowed so much water that I spat up all the carbolic acid—and you know, if I hadn't been such a darn good swimmer, I would've drowned.

The Insect Powder Agent

"How're you doin', Henry?"

"I'm in a new business."

"What's the new business?"

"I'm an agent."

"An agent for what?"

"Insect powder."

"Insect powder?"

"Do you want to buy some of my powder?"

"I know I don't want any insect powder."

"It's mighty nice powder."

"I said I didn't want any powder."

"Good day, sir. Good day."

"Good day, Henry . . . Ah, just a moment."

"I knew you wanted some of this insect powder."

"No, I hardly think I need any; but, just how is this powder used?"

"Very simple, very simple. I'll try and tell you how to use it. You get up about four or three o'clock in the mornin', when your place is quiet and still, with a lamp in your right hand and some powder in the other. You sneak down the stairs in your stocking feet till you get to the kitchen. Then you look all around till you see a roach or a bug, and when you see a bug, you flash the lamp in the bug's eyes till you hypnotize it."

"What—hypnotize a bug?"

"Then you take him five or four times around the room until the bug sweats, until he's all exhausted. Then you stoop down, grab him by the back of the neck between the forefinger and the thumb, and you choke him until he is black in the face."

"What are you tryin' to tell me?"

"Then you take a shovelful of this powder, and you ram it down that bug's throat. And when you get him full of powder, you slam him down on the floor, jump on him until the bug is dead."

"I should've been on my way long ago. Good day, Henry, good day."

The Instant Tent

"I'm lookin' for a tent."

"Here is your new instant model."

"Instant model?"

"Yes, it comes freeze-dried and fits in your hip pocket. You drop it in a pail of water and it will fill right out to a three-man tent."

"Yes, but I'd be afraid if it rained all night, you might wake up the next mornin' in the center of a three-ring circus, and once it swelled up, how do you get it to shrink down again so you can break camp?"

"You leave it in the sun for an hour."

"Yes, and if you oversleep, you end up back inside your own hip pocket."

The Bear and the Slicker

A city slicker was asked to go hunting with a group of Maine sports. When the slicker said he could not bring himself to kill a harmless deer, they gave him a squirrel gun and told him to go off and find a bear.

He struck off bravely into the woods, and before ten minutes were gone, he come upon what he was looking for. He dropped his gun and tore back to camp with a bear close on his heels. The slicker tripped on the cabin door sill, and the bear tripped on him, rolling head over heels into the cabin.

The slicker collected himself, dashed outside the cabin, slammed the door, and, peering in the open window, shouted, "There's your bear, fellas! You skin him out while I go back for more!"

Conversation on a Train

"One way or round-trip?"

"Round trip."

"Where to?"

"Right back here, I guess."

"Conductor, why have we stopped so soon after leaving the station?"

" 'Cause of the cattle on the tracks ahead."

"Conductor, why have we stopped again?"

"We caught up to them cows again."

"This train should have a cow catcher on the rear to protect us from overtaking cattle."

"Yes, Mr. Conductor, this is surely the slowest train I've ever been on. Now, that train from Portland there—there was a train. Pulled out so fast, I kissed a cow goodbye instead of my wife."

"You don't like this train? Why don't you get off and walk?"

"I would, but my folks are not expecting me till the train pulls in. How come the train is runnin' so smoothly now, Mr. Conductor?"

"We have jumped the track."

The Clam Quartet

You never heard about them singing clams of mine. Well now, let me tell ya.

Three years ago, I was clammin' over to Dougal Flats. I set my bucket in a likely spot and begun to dig. All at onc't, I heard sort of a low hummin' sound. I looked over and found it was comin' from the mud. Dug down, and found it was clams that was doin' it.

Now, since I used to play sliphorn in the Penobscot Chowder Band, I knew somethin' about music and about how you go about formin' up a quartet.

By diggin' up more than a hundred of them clams, I got four that harmonized. I filled a box with gravel and mud from the same clam flat, and packed them clams in it so's they might feel at home, even in captivity. I'd lift 'em out at feedin' time and rub their little stomachs so they'd open up and hum for me.

One day, when the alto clam hummed a tune, I rewarded him with some extra chopped liver and bacon. And it weren't long before the others caught on and begun to sing along in harmony.

You know, I took them clams all over this country, on a road tour. They had engagements in New York, Chicago—all

the big cities. But I shall rue the day I signed a contract for a European tour. Took the five finest staterooms on the *Queen Mary*, but before we even got to Nantucket Lightship, where there was ever so slight a swell, them poor little fellas, to a clam, up took seasick, and died.

Bert and I . . .

Birth Control

Henry Whipple called the doctor as soon as his wife begun to have contractions. He got the pitchers of hot water and the towels ready, and the doctor asked Henry to hold up the lantern as he delivered the child.

Just as the doctor was washing up to go home, the contractions started again.

"Hold up the lantern, Henry," he said.

And the doctor delivered a baby girl.

"Wait, Henry, wait—hold up that lantern so I can see here."

And the doctor delivered another girl.

"What are you doin', blowin' out the lantern, Henry?" asked the doctor.

"The light's drawin' 'em," Henry replied.

Harry Whitfield Flies to New York

Harry Whitfield left the breakfast table early. He told his wife, Margaret, that he had to go out and sharpen his axe. Then he decided the grindstone was worn down too far, and he'd have to go up to Bangor to get a new one. He climbed into his Model A sedan and headed up to Bangor to Reynolds' Hardware. Harry'd had to make all his trips to Bangor by car instead of rail ever since the Boston and Maine discontinued passenger service on the Tunk Lake spur.

By the time Harry'd paid his dime at the Bangor Bridge, it was so foggy he could hardly see ten feet in front of him. Harry missed a right turn down into the business district and continued on out onto Hammond Street toward the Bangor International Airport. He failed to notice the dead end sign, and rode up over the curb onto a strip of grass that let out onto what seemed to him to be a ten-lane highway lit up on either side by the nicest amber lights.

Harry just headed right down the middle until he saw a truck behind, trying to pass him—or at least he thought it was a truck. It was the widest truck with the brightest headlights he'd ever seen. Harry had just started pulling over to the right when that truck commenced to run right over Harry. His head was snapped back and pinned there, and he felt the whole car lift right off the ground.

Little did Harry realize that he'd been scooped into the wheel well of a departing 747.

Harry couldn't make out where he was; it was dark and windy and cold, and he figured maybe he was having another one of his spells. It wasn't until his hearing aid somehow picked up the captain of the 747 making speeches that Harry began to understand what had happened.

The plane was soon to land at John F. Kennedy Airfield, and Harry knew he'd be deposited on the runway at way over the speed limit. Harry tested the brakes and the steering wheel of his Model A.

"Hope them leaf springs don't buckle on me," said Harry.

When Harry touched down, things went by in such a blur that he had to drive for a while on instruments. The speedometer went around three times, but the car was slowed by some bulrushes and a chain-link fence, so that by the time he shot out onto the Van Wyck Expressway, he was only going forty-five.

Four days later and seven tire changes, Harry was back in Bangor, buying a grinding wheel.

When he reached home that night, his wife Margaret was waitin' at the door for him with a rollin' pin.

"Well, Margaret," said Harry, "that axe sure was some dull."

Cutler Harbor

Cutler Harbor . . . you ask me about Cutler Harbor. That's where I was born and raised. Lived there all my days, man and boy, following the sea; well, I say, following the sea. I ain't never done much blue-water sailin', mostly just coastin'. I've got me a little jib 'n' mainsail boat, the *Nancy and Betsy,* and me and my nephew Willie 'n' me, we runs it, we don't carry no hands—we don't need no hands. Though the mainsail is heavy for Willie 'n' me; we just ease the peak and let the mainsail flap.

Well now, you'd've thought we'da known every ripple and reef from here to Eastport and back again; but then again, I recollect that time we was takin' on a deckload of lumber for transportin' off to Ram Island. We got in off Goat Head there, when there come a hail from shore. It seems they was havin' a hair-settin' party—what you might call a christenin'. Well, we put in close up under the head and we dropped anchor; we lowered the jib, but we didn't have to lower the mainsail. The mainsail was heavy for Willie 'n' me, so we just eased the peak and let the mainsail flap.

Well, we went ashore there, and when I tell ya that they had two barrels of Barbados rum jacked up there on the beach, you'll understand me when I tell ya that they were partin' the baby's hair good and proper. Well, after a while, Willie, he started partin' a few hairs himself. And I said, "Willie, if we're gonna get off on this tide, we better get a move on."

So we went back aboard the *Nancy and Betsy,* we weighed anchor, we raised the jib, but we didn't have to raise the mainsail, because you see, we hadn't lowered the mainsail. The mainsail had been heavy for Willie 'n' me, so we had just eased the peak and let the mainsail flap. Well, we raised the peak and we set sail outta there, and gone for no more than five minutes when there come in one of them fogs you get around Cutler, so thick you can't see your nose in front of your face.

And I said, "Willie, where be we?"

He says, "I don't know."

"Well," I said, "Willie you better go belowdecks and bring up that Coastwise Pilot."

He brung it up on deck, and it were a tattered edition, and he no sooner got it open to the Cutler page when there come along a little puff of wind—just a zephyr—and blew that page right overboard.

I said, "Willie, what are we gonna do now?"

He said, "I don't know."

"Well," I said, "I think we'd better ponder."

So we dropped anchor, we lowered the jib, but we didn't have to lower the mainsail. The mainsail was heavy for Willie 'n me, so we just eased the peak and let the mainsail flap, and then, oh my Lord, how we did ponder. First, Willie pondered; then I pondered. We took turns a'ponderin', and then all at once, it come to me.

I said, "Willie, I got it! I tell you what we're gonna do— we're gonna weigh anchor, we're gonna raise the jib, we're gonna raise the peak, we're gonna set sail outta here, and we're gonna keep a'sailin', by Godfrey mighty, until we get over into this next page here! And then we'll know where we be!"

A Fella Just Can't Never Get Away from the Sea

You know, a fella just can't never get away from the sea. I've tried from time to time, but I never did get away from the sea for very long. A fella just can't never get away from the sea.

Now, I shall never forget that time I was rakin' leaves on one of them cold, raw, foggy days you get along the coast of Maine, and Mr. Smith come out and asked me if I'd like to get warmed up by the fire and have a little somethin' to drink.

"Well," I said, "Mr. Smith, I'd like first-rate to get warm, but if it's all the same to you, I'll not have anything to drink—I haven't had anything to drink for over thirty-five years, Mr. Smith," I said. "But I recollect just like it was yesterday that last time I partook of spirits. I was building boats in them days, and I was also building coffins. I built most of the coffins that them folks are buried in up on the hill, and I'd just finished a catboat for Henry Furness's boy when Charlie Pierce come over. He run the general store and did the undertaking on the side. He said, 'I've got to have me a coffin by Thursday.'

"I said, 'Charlie, it's short notice.' He said, 'I know it is, so I've brung you over a jug of Jamaica rum.' Well, I didn't spare myself none, nor may I say did I spare that rum, and Wednesday night I went to bed feeling pretty good—very good. And proud of a job well done.

"In the morning Charlie come over and I showed him out to the shed, and I noticed he kind of started some as we walked through the door of that shed, and there that coffin stood— and it had a rudder and a centerboard on it!

A fella just can't never get away from the sea.

Aunt Mehitabel

And then there was Aunt Mehitabel, bless her heart. She was a card from a long line of cards, she was. And she said she was gonna get out to California before she died. Well, she just made it.

Well, she got out there and she wired us that she'd had a very pleasant trip to California, that she'd gone by way of Bangor, but that she did not like California on account of it was so far from the ocean. And she said she was heading back east as fast as she could.

Well, she got on the train and got as far as Sacramento when she come down with the collywobbles and on top of that, the tizzick. The collywobbles will fell an ox, but it took the tizzick to drop Aunt Mehitabel. She passed away on the train, and we wired the stationmaster to crate her up and ship her east.

And she arrived five days later at Cutler siding. We rushed her through the funeral services. . . . It was the middle of August.

Then we got her out to the graveyard and was about to lower her away when curiosity got the best of us and we pried up a board to have a last look-see, and there, inside, was an admiral in full dress uniform. Making the best of an unsettling situation, we lowered the admiral and buried him quick, in the hopes that somewhere, Aunt Mehitabel would be gettin' a twenty-one-gun salute.

The Balloon and the Stove

Hetty and me decided to try and get as far away from the sea as we could. So we headed inland and settled on a little farm not far from Skowhegan. And she, bein' a farm girl, said, "You know, Virgie, plant early, harvest early when you're in this business."

Well, it weren't long before she gave birth to a baby boy.

Well, she said that he was some cunnin', but you know, you could've got me a sharp knife and a soft piece of white pine and I could have whittled you a better-lookin' baby than the one we got.

He come out weighin' three pounds, five ounces.

Hetty says, "I barely got my bait back!"

Well, you know it was nothin' but mud and frost, frost and mud. As soon as the frost'd end in the spring, the mud'd commence, and it wouldn't stop until the frost commenced in the fall.

Hetty and me, we headed even further inland. We did this by going to the Skowhegan Fair where they had an ascension of a lighter-than-air balloon on the last day, and we got right up close to that balloon, jumped aboard the gondola, and they loosed the lines. We were up out of sight before they could do anything about it.

The wind blew us westward; we saw a farmer plowin' in the field, and I cried out, "Where are we?"

He didn't even look up, he just said, "You're in a balloon, ya damn fools!"

Well, the wind carried us even further inland until we come to the woods of Maine, and I saw a clearing, let the gas out of the balloon, come down light as a feather.

I didn't waste no time. I built a cabin in the woods and then I hauled some old oil drums from a nearby railroad siding, and I welded and soldered 'em together as best I could, and come up with a stove that was a strange-looking contraption. The draft hole come in the top and the stovepipe went out the bottom; but, you know, I knew that that stove was gonna have one heck of a draft.

And some of the local guide fellas come over and they laughed at that stove, and they laughed at me. But I warned 'em that that stove was gonna have one heck of a draft, and they'd better stand back when it started up.

I went off to the woodshed to fetch an armload of hardwood that would burn slow and easy—I didn't want to have no nuclear reaction.

Well, sir, I was headin' back toward the cabin when the most awful roarin' sound started up.

"Who put soft wood in that stove? You put kindlin' in it, you started it up, and it's goin' much too strong, ya damn fools!"

Well, I had a hard time gettin' back into that cabin. I had to grip the sides of the door frame such was the suction comin' out of that stove. And them guide fellas was holdin' onto the insides of that cabin with their teeth and fingernails dug right into the walls, and their legs a'flappin' in midair.

Well, there was a clatter, an awful clatter, and first the lid-lifter and then the stoker and then the shovel was sucked right in through the draft and rattled out of the chimney. And then there was an awful wrench and that stove lifted up off the cabin floor and come to rest against the splits of the roof. I said "come to rest"—it weren't but a minute 'fore there was another ungodly wrench, and the cabin lifted right up off its foundations.

Well, I knew right then and there, we had a stove with one heck of a draft!

I got up on top of a chair and grabbed a'hold of that damper handle and with great presence of mind, I ever-so-slowly turned that damper handle toward the "closed" position, thereby easing the cabin back down to its foundations, and ever so gentle, lowering the stove back down to the cabin floor. I turned the damper all the way off, shut the draft; the roaring subsided, and one of them fool guides who had returned to the upright—he had the audacity to say, "You know, Virgie, if you had had a governor on that stove, then that wouldn't've happened."

I said, "Governor, heck—you put soft wood in that stove and not even the president of the United States is gonna hold it down!"

Beginner's Luck

Well, suh, fella's got to know how to shoot a gun if he's gonna be a Maine guide, and I asked one of them local fellas to come over and give me instructions. He brung over an old rusted-out .22 squirrel gun, and he said, "Virgie—you see them tracks at your feet?" He said, "Them is rabbit tracks, and at the end of 'em is your breakfast."

"Well," I said, "I thought you were gonna show me how to shoot this gun."

He said, "Experience is the best teacher. Now, go to it, Virgie."

And he struck me on the back and I staggered off into the woods, following them rabbit tracks. Now I hadn't gone more than a hundred yards before I come to the side of a hill and I heard a roaring sound. It was a bear, comin' up after me. And I heard a screechin', and it was a mountain lion comin' down after me.

Well, I determined to take the bear on first. And he come at me with his mouth wide open, and I put my back to a tree and I stood my ground. There he was; he come closer, and I stuck my hand right into his mouth and down his throat, through his intestines, and out the other side.

Well, then I grabbed a'hold of his tail and I gave one heck of a yank, and pulled that bear right inside out.

'Course, that bear kept a'goin', but it was in the other direction.

Now, at just that moment, the mountain lion was almost on me when we heard a pack of wolves, closin' in on the two of us. I looked at the mountain lion and he looked at me, and we figured that whatever our differences was, we'd take the wolves on first.

I no sooner got the stockade built when them wolves was on us, and there was a great, tremendous battle, and inside of ten minutes, all them wolves were killed.

And I looked at the mountain lion and he looked at me, and we figured that whatever our troubles was, they was over, and he turned on his heels, walked back up on the hill; I turned on my heels, walked down the hill, followin' them rabbit tracks.

Now I hadn't gone more than another hundred yards before I come to the side of a stream, and I was about to ford that stream when I spied two foxes on the opposite bank. They was foamin' at the mouth, and their eyes were startin' out of their heads, and I could see they had rabies, and they were gonna bite me if they could.

So I drew a bead, right in between them two foxes—I didn't know which one to fire at—and I was about to squeeze off the last round when I heard a honkin' sound. I looked up overhead and there was twelve wild geese, a'headin' south, and I heard a quackin'—there was twelve wild ducks, a'headin' north. Well, I was sore tempted to fire at them birds, but I determined to take the danger on first, and I squeezed off the last round.

The gun exploded in my face. It was rusted-out, as you will remember. Now the butt of the gun flew north and knocked down all twelve ducks. The barrel of the gun flew south and skewered all twelve geese. The bullet sped true to its mark, struck a rock, split it in two, and killed both foxes. The kick of the explosion was such as to knock me into the stream behind, and when I come to, my right hand was on an otter's head, my left hand was on a beaver's tail, and my trouser pockets were so full of trout that a button popped off my fly and killed the rabbit.

That's what you might call "beginner's luck."

About the Storytellers

Marshall "Mike" Dodge stands undeniably as a godfather of Down East humor, bringing an energy and imagination to the stage that took him from a small Connecticut studio to his standing as the premier New England humorist of his era before he was tragically killed by a hit-and-run driver in Hawaii in 1982. He was just 45. Mike was born in New York, attended high school in New Hampshire (where he first heard "Down East humor"), and graduated from Yale, where he studied philosophy. It was at Yale in 1958 that he and Bob Bryan cut the first "Bert and I" album and launched what is now a Maine icon.

Robert Bryan helped launch "Bert and I" with Dodge in part by drawing upon his memories from childhood summers spent at his beloved Tunk Lake, where he was fascinated by the area's stories and storytellers. Like Dodge, Bob was born and raised in New York and graduated from Yale. Unlike Dodge, who continued as full-time performer, Rev. Robert A. Bryan used earnings from the early records in the 1960s to help launch and grow another dream—the Quebec-Labrador Foundation, which provides support to remote communities mainly in Quebec and Labrador. Bob continues as a major force at QLF and remains involved in the continued life of "Bert and I."

Discography

BERT AND I . . .
And Other Stories from Down East

The iconic "Bert and I" stories were first created by Yale University students Marshall Dodge and Robert Bryan in the late 1950s and performed around campus. The two amateur storytellers soon recorded a short 10-inch album of eleven stories for friends and family, but ultimately pressed just a few hundred. This rare album is the first "Bert and I" recording.

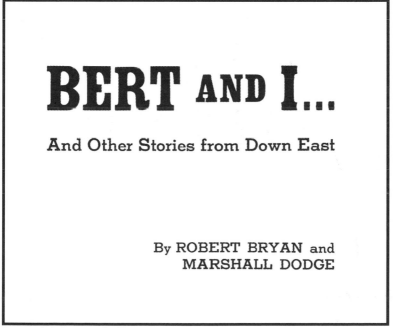

BERT AND I...

And Other Stories from Down East

By ROBERT BRYAN and
MARSHALL DODGE

Private label, 10-inch album

BERT AND I . . . And Other Stories from Down East

The growing popularity of Dodge and Bryan and the relative success of their initial 10-inch album prompted them in 1958 to record and release the seminal commercial album of New England humor and storytelling—*Bert and I . . . And Other Stories from Down East*. Featuring nineteen stories, the album depicted Maine fishermen and woodsmen with dry, classic

Album, Bert and I, Inc., 1958

humor and set the tone and direction of the genre for decades. It was also notable for taking a sometimes risque or ribald genre as it existed in its oral format and moving it into the mainstream.

SIDE ONE
1. Bert and I
2. Kenneth Fowler Goes Hunting
3. Camden Pierce Goes to New York
4. The Sassage
5. The Lighter-than-air Balloon
6. Which Way to East Vassalboro?
7. Which Way to Millinocket?
8. The Long Hill
9. The Liar
10. Mad Dog

SIDE TWO
1. Down East Socialism
2. Down East Religion
3. Albert's Moose
4. Virgil Bliss
5. Chester Coombs' First-born
6. Arnold Bunker Testifies
7. The Body in the Kelp
8. The Long Fezzle
9. Harry Whitfield's Trip

FROM THE ALBUM JACKET NOTES:
It's hard to say which is more charming, the culture of rural northern New England or the art of telling about it. In point of time, the one is as old as the other, for the Yankee's

monumental pride-of-place has always found expression in oral, anecdotal form. Even the late, learned Wilbur Cross once observed that he had absorbed his proud New England heritage "not from books, but from the lips of men and women." The medium of the yarn has traditionally been favored to the essay or the verse, and only partly because the demands of the latter generally exceeded the formal book-learning of the native; the Down East story has in telling a warmth and a pace and an accent which are beyond the dimensions of the printed page.

In *Bert and I . . . And Other Stories from Down East*, two young men, hardly old enough to have absorbed the culture in its totality, but with an instinct for the telling of it, have combined forces to bring a taste of northern New England into homes everywhere. They have chosen to tell anecdotes accentuating Yankee humor (a decision that reflects popular judgement) but in doing so they have also managed to illuminate a good many aspects of the New England character. The sea and the land— the two most important facts of life in New England—are here, along with the general store, the city-slicker who has lost his way, and a number of other more or less standard props. But chiefly the Messrs. Dodge and Bryan have given the listener the soft accent, the easy pace, the literalness, and the homely wisdom of the New England native. They have dramatized the parsimony, in both word and deed, of the descendants of "Brother Johnathan." Having invested their characters with the trappings of the rustic they have nonetheless taken care to insure—as in all New England folklore—that the simple wit and wisdom of the Yankee comes out best.

Quite apart from their contribution to the preservation and promotion of a kind of folk art, the creators of this record have made an impressive debut as entertainers. Capitalizing on a youth spent at the figurative knee of the Down East lobstermen and "hired hands," both demonstrate mastery of the art of sympathetic caricature. And what may be equally impressive, they have recreated some of the sounds of their setting, using their throats and tongues alone.

—Homer Babbidge, 1958

Bert and I . . . And Other Stories from Down East

In 2009, more than fifty years after its release, the stories told on the milestone *Bert and I* album were digitally remastered to create a special CD edition, which also includes three stories taken from the privately produced 10-inch album that preceded the first commercial record. These three stories either did not

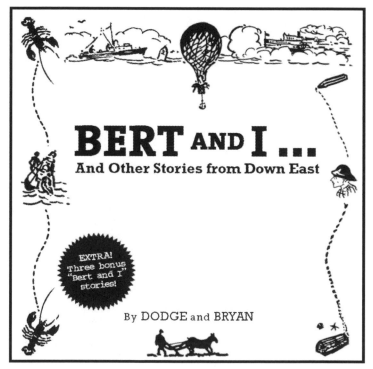

CD, Islandport Press, Inc.

appear on the commercial album or were changed. For example, the original and now legendary first "Bert and I" story did change and both versions are included on this CD.

1. Bert and I
2. Kenneth Fowler Goes Hunting
3. Camden Pierce Goes to New York
4. The Sassage
5. The Lighter-than-air Balloon
6. Which Way to East Vassalboro?
7. Which Way to Millinocket?
8. The Long Hill
9. The Liar
10. Mad Dog
11. Down East Socialism
12. Down East Religion
13. Albert's Moose
14. Virgil Bliss
15. Chester Coombs' First-born
16. Arnold Bunker Testifies
17. The Body in the Kelp
18. The Long Fezzle
19. Harry Whitfield's Trip
Bonus: Bert and I (Alt.)
Bonus: Effie and the Iron Lung
Bonus: A Fair Trade

MORE BERT AND I . . . And
Other Stories from Down East

In the 1960s, Dodge and Bryan built on the success of *Bert and I . . . And Other Stories from Down East* with *More Bert and I . . . .* The album includes the classic story, "The Plane Ride," and marks the return of Virgil Bliss, who appears on the first album.

Album, Bert and I, Inc.

From the album jacket notes:

The public attached to "Bert and I" ever since their first recording in 1958 will be glad to know that these two narrators of Northern New England folklore are with us again. Dialect and sound effects are as authentic and startling as before.

The stories are either new or they are variations on older themes. Those of us whose hearts sank when the *Bluebird I* out of Kennebunkport was run down by the *Bangor Packet*, are treated, as promised, to a ride on the *Bluebird II*. This time it's not fog and a steamboat, but a frog-man and lobsters of which the *Bluebird* runs afoul. Essie Fickett rides again in her ferrous vehicle and there's a new dog by the name of Blue who trots into the narrative. The longest yarn is a lament for the demise of the "choo-choo," calculated to wring the withers of the staunchest railroad buff.

In these days of turbulence in world affairs we need to be reminded that crisis between the people and their environment have always been the order of the day since Man was ushered out of Eden. With so much contrived humor abroad, smacking more of the boudoir than the barnyard, it's good to be exposed to an authentic brand of wit, where a spade is a shovel and not a bridge-hand, and a privy is a sanctuary and not a household appliance and a plumber's delight.

My friend Homer Babbidge, a storyteller of accomplishment like his Greek namesake, first introduced "Bert and I" to the listening public. Now at their invitation and with some comparative trepidation, I follow in succession. In their "store clothes" "Bert and I" are The Reverend Robert Bryan, Chaplain of the Choate School, Wallingford, Connecticut, and Marshall Dodge, who is pursuing his studies in philosophy at Boston University. I first met them when they were undergraduates at Yale. As a matter of fact, when I was University Chaplain and Professor of Bible Literature, I set them both "doing chores" on Mother Yale's farm in New Haven. The boys did right well then and have been so doing ever since. In proof of this, I suggest you get acquainted with their second original recording and you'll understand what I mean.

—Uncle Sid Lovett

More album jacket notes:

Alan Bemis supplied many of the ideas and phrases of the first story, "More Bert and I." "The Government Fly" is entirely his story. His stories also appear in "The Lament of Age "and "The Return of Virgil," as do the stories of the Vermont poet, Walter Hard. Alan Bemis and Walter Hard are the most discriminating grass roots collectors of New England humor today. As secondary collectors, we are deeply indebted to them. David Tirrell supplied the story, "The Iron Lung." "President Harding" is a verbatim retelling of the story as it appears on our record, *A Maine Pot-Hellion* as told by Walter Kilham. Despite our rendition, the story still stands as a classic. The designer of the cover, Nelson C. White, supplied us with the idea for "The Little Gull." He in turn derived the idea from his readings of E.B. White.

BERT AND I /
MORE BERT AND I

In the 1990s, all the stories from the first two albums were included on a single CD produced by Bert and I, Inc. In the 2000s, the stories on this double CD were digitally remastered for improved sound quality and the CD was rereleased by Islandport Press.

CD, Islandport Press, Inc.

THE RETURN OF BERT AND I:
How the Bluebird II plugged the hole in the Machias Maru, thus saving the coast of Maine . . . and other stories

In the early 1970s, Dodge and Bryan teamed up for a third album. This one includes "Directions," "Gagnon, World Champion Moose Caller," and "The Stove with the Powerful Draft." By this time, Dodge was fully engaged in a multi-faceted

Album, Bert and I, Inc.

live performing career and even starred in a television series, "A Downeast Smile-In," that aired on Maine Public Television. "Gagnon" and "The Stove with the Powerful Draft" were among the stories that would move with him from studio to stage, although they were adapted for live performance. The notes on the album state that Dodge "is presently hard at work trying to master vaudeville monologues, circus and carnival barks, medicine show spiels, the art of declamation, and the candy pitch." Meanwhile, Bob Bryan was devoting his time to the Quebec Labrador Mission Foundation. The initial sales of the duo's first album had allowed him to buy a floatplane in the 1960s and begin a career as a flying minister for the Anglican Church of Canada in isolated areas in the North.

SIDE ONE
1. The Return of Bert and I
2. Directions
3. Gagnon, World Champion Moose Caller
4. The Return of Virgil Bliss
5. Harry Sleeps at L.L. Bean's

SIDE TWO
1. By a Fluke
2. The Silent Chain Saw
3. M'am Hackett's Compost Heap
4. At the Graveyard
5. The Stove with a Powerful Draft
6. The Captain and the Lady
7. The Chicken Truck
8. Harry Startles Wiscasset

FROM THE ALBUM JACKET NOTES:

"The Return of Bert and I." The first tale on this record was inspired by the story of the Texaco tanker, *Tamano* which, on July 22, 1972, rounded a buoy in Portland harbor too closely and struck a ledge, tearing a twenty–foot gash in her bottom and spilling 100,000 gallons of oil into the water. It was also inspired by the tale of the little Dutch boy. The characters of "Bert and I" were born in the imagination of John Cochran.

"Directions" is a folk dialogue found in many regions of this country. It is strikingly similar to the Arkansas traveler dialogue.

"Gagnon" is an adaptation of "The Champeen Moose Caller" found in a book, *Beyond the Sowdyhunk* by Stanley Foss Bartlett. James Garvin has helped greatly with the style of the story.

"The Return of Virgil Bliss" reintroduces a character from the first two records and was born in the imagination of John Cochran.

"Harry Sleeps at L.L. Bean's" reintroduces Harry Whitfield—whose long trip to New York from Tunk Lake and back is recounted in the first two "Bert and I" records. In this story, he suffers from a seemingly incurable case of driver's sleeping sickness.

"By a Fluke" is the encounter of Bert and I with a whale, suggested by Joseph Chase Allen's writings in the *Vineyard Gazette*.

"The Silent Chain Saw" is a modern folk story made into a dialogue.

"M'am Hackett's Compost Heap" is told in countless versions throughout the nineteenth century American nautical literature.

"At the Graveyard" is a series of typical New England two-line jokes about burial, all grouped together here for the first time.

"The Stove with the Powerful Draft" is a tall story made famous by Ed Grant, the well-known Rangeley Lakes guide.

"The Captain and the Lady" is another series of two-line jokes focusing upon a Maine ferryboat captain and an "outsider."

"The Chicken Truck" is probably an updated vaudeville joke.

"Harry Startles Wiscasset" is inspired by a true anecdote of a man who really did tumble out of his camper—naked—onto the Main street of Wiscasset.

BERT AND I Stem Inflation, and Other Stories

Also in the 1970s, Dodge and Bryan released their fourth and final original "Bert and I" album. Both would record other albums, but not together. Notable stories on this album include "Frost, You Say," which Dodge also released as a book, and "Too

Album, Bert and I, Inc.

Late, Mr. Perkins." Interestingly, an optional title for this album that was rejected was "Bert and I Solve the Energy Crisis."

SIDE ONE
1. Bert and I Stem Inflation
2. No News
3. The Bear in the Spring
4. The Pet Turkey
5. Too Late, Mr. Perkins
6. Texas vs. Maine
7. Frost, You Say
8. Tom Rawls
9. Life Insurance
10. Lewis Bayard and the Judge
11. Dog Lover
12. Bert and I and the Bricks

SIDE TWO
1. Bert and I Solve the Energy Crisis
2. Buryin'
3. The Whole Load
4. Suicide
5. The Insect Powder Agent
6. Cutler Harbor
7. The Instant Tent
8. The Bear and the Slicker
9. Conversation on a Train
10. The Clam Quartet
11. Birth Control
12. Bottle Squatting
13. Harry Whitfield Flies to New York

"No News" is an old vaudeville classic performed by Nat Wills and others. "Too Late" is a story given to us by the late great Horace Stevens, along with "Frost, You Say" and "Cutler Harbor." "The Bricks" we got from Alan Bemis. "Suicide" is a story Arthur Bryan found on an old "78." "The Insect Powder Agent" is from Golden and Marlow via John Cowles' great record collection. "The Instant Teeth" was given to us by Sandy Ives. The beginning and ending of the "Harry Whitfield" story were given to us by Ken Morse. "Bert and I Solve the Energy Crisis" is a steal from the Kennebeck Mariner by Holman Day.

Alternate cover proposed for Bert and I Stem Inflation

THE RETURN OF BERT AND I /
BERT AND I Stem Inflation

In the 1990s, all the stories from the third and fourth albums were included on a single CD by Bert and I, Inc. In the 2000s, the stories on this double CD were digitally remastered for improved sound quality and the CD was rereleased by Islandport Press.

CD, Islandport Press, Inc.

BERT AND I . . . ON STAGE: MARSHALL DODGE
in performance

This wonderful album was created from a live performance that Marshall Dodge gave at the University of Maine in Orono in 1977. Among other things, it shows how well Dodge adapted

Album, Bert and I, Inc.

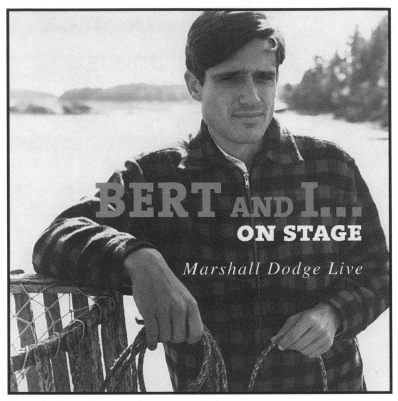

CD, Islandport Press, Inc.

the "Bert and I" stories—often merging stories and dialogues together to create new versions of the material—for the stage. It also clearly demonstrates his growth as a live performer. The stories on the album and an initial CD were digitally remastered in the 2000s and re-released by Islandport Press, Inc.

CONTENTS (AS LISTED ON THE ISLANDPORT CD)
1. Plant Early, Harvest Early
2. Lighter than Air Balloon
3. One Heckuva Draft

4. Beginner's Luck
5. Bear in the Spring
6. Gagnon
7. Can't Get Away from the Sea
8. Cutler Harbor
9. Coffin with a Centerboard
10. Aunt Mehitable
11. Set'er Again
12. Bert and I

FROM THE ALBUM JACKET NOTES:

Marshall Dodge, III, was a philosopher, folklorist and devotee of the arts. He started telling Maine stories in 1953 when John Cochran introduced him to the imaginary lobster-fishermen, Bert and I. At Yale, Dodge combined repertoires with fellow raconteur and friend, Robert Bryan, and together they produced *Bert and I . . . And Other Stories From Down East*. This brought instant success and they formed the Bert and I Corporation. A series of recordings followed.

Dodge was killed in a hit-and-run accident while bicycling in Hawaii in January 1982. At the time of his death he was at the height of his popularity as America's premier New England humorist. The *Bert and I* recordings and subsequent book have become a part of his legacy.

In 1977, he conceived and produced the Maine Festival of the Arts which takes place at Bowdoin College each summer to celebrate the arts and crafts of Maine—his adopted state.

Dodge's partner, Robert Bryan, an Episcopal clergyman, continues to fly an airplane between Maine and the Atlantic Provinces of Canada—coordinating educational programs for the Quebec Labrador Foundation, which he started in 1961. Bryan has plans for future recordings on the "Bert and I" label.

This recording, using many stories from the original *Bert and I* record, was made before an audience at the University of Maine in Orono in the fall of 1977. For stories on this record thanks go to Alan Bemis, Walter Kilham, James Garvin, Horace Stevens, John Cochran, Robert Bryan, Kendall Morse, Holman Day, and Stanley Foss Bartlett. Mark Andres, who illustrated the book, *Bert and I . . . And Other Stories from Down East*, is the album artist. Lynn Franklin is the photographer.

A Downeast Smile-In

This DVD contains three episodes of Marshall Dodge's original *A Downeast Smile-In* series, first broadcast on Maine Educational Television in 1970.

FROM THE DVD JACKET NOTES:
"I am going to tell you some Maine stories. Some of them have been told to me. Some I have come upon in books. And some I have made up myself. All of the stories reflect the spirit of "old" Maine. And all are stories, not jokes. They end gently with a poke rather than a punch. And most have messages that live on through many tellings."
—Marshall Dodge

DVD, Northeast Historic Film

THE BEST OF BERT AND I . . . :
Celebrating 50 Years of Stories from Down East

To celebrate the 50th Anniversary of the original *Bert and I* album, Islandport Press produced a special commemorative CD in 2008 featuring thirty-four stories selected from the four Dodge and Bryan albums, Dodge's live album, and Dodge's *A Downeast Smile-In.* All tracks were digitally remastered for improved sound quality.

1. Bert and I
2. Which Way to Millinocket?
3. The Liar
4. The Body in the Kelp
5. Mad Dog
6. Arnold Bunker Testifies
7. Down East Socialism
8. By a Fluke
9. Directions
10. The Chicken Truck
11. The Silent Chain Saw
12. Gagnon
13. Bear in the Spring
14. Texas vs. Maine
15. The Captain and the Lady
16. Birth Control
17. Virgil Bliss
18. Too Late, Mr. Perkins
19. Camden Pierce Goes to New York

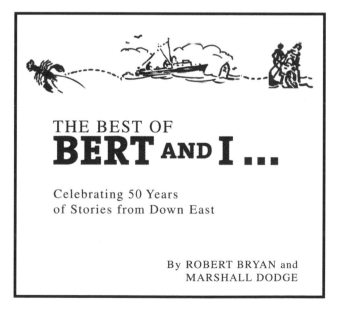

THE BEST OF
BERT AND **I ...**

Celebrating 50 Years
of Stories from Down East

By ROBERT BRYAN and
MARSHALL DODGE

CD, Islandport Press, Inc.

A Maine Pot-Hellion

In addition to being a performing duo, "Bert and I" was also a record label. The label produced several records in the 1960s. In the 1980s, the label produced the early recordings of Tim Sample. One of the label's most popular early albums that featured storytellers other than Dodge and Bryan was *A Maine Pot-Hellion*. It also includes a seeming rarity for that era, a recorded female Down East storyteller. A CD version of this classic album is planned for 2012.

SIDE ONE

    Frost, You Say? by Horace Stevens
    Mud Time by Alan Bemis
    Unc by Steve Graham
    Ethel by Betty Brown
    Barbados Rum by Horace Stevens
    The Whole Darned Necessary by Alan Bemis
    The She-Bear by Peter Kilham

SIDE TWO

    Old Diamond by Lawrence Kilham
    The Dead Air Pocket by Lawrence Kilham
    Up She Comes by Peter Kilham
    Kench's Mountain by George Allen
    President Harding by Walter Kilham
    The Great Tremenjous Tiger by Walter Kilham
    Cutler Harbor by Horace Stevens
    Harvey Garmage by William Lippincott
    Emma Condon by Alan Bemis

In March of 1959, Alan Bemis and "Bert and I" gathered the best Down East storytellers they could find. From that session came the first side of this record, which, at the suggestion of Peter Kilham, was tied together by the device of a postman making his rounds. No one could have done the postman better than Peter himself.

Steve Graham and George Allen are both natives of Brooklin, Maine, and are the only two people on the record who escape the "summer visitor" category.

Album, Bert and I, Inc.

The late Horace Stevens was well known for his storytelling as "Mr. Puckins" before the Sangerfest and the St. Botolph Club and other such groups in Cambridge and Boston.

Betty Caffee Brown (Mrs. Phelps Brown) divides her time between Florida and Deer Isle, Maine.

The three Kilham brothers gathered in Tamworth, New Hampshire, for a verbal portrait which occupies much of Side Two. Walter is retired and living in Cornwall, Connecticut. Lawrence resides in Lyme, New Hampshire, and is doing independent research on birds. Peter is busy being president of Droll Yankees, Inc. in Foster, Rhode Island.

William Lippincott, former dean of students at Princeton University, has semi-retired to Northeast Harbor, Maine.

The album cover is the work of Nelson White of Waterford, Connecticut, who is a master raconteur in his own right.

To Alan Bemis goes much of the credit for making this record possible. He selected the title (a "pot-hellion" is a Maine stew) and gathered most of the raconteurs.

Other Bert and I-related Albums & Books

All four Dodge and Bryan albums, as well as Dodge's *Bert and I On Stage,* were released as cassettes.

Cassette

Frost, You Say?: Yankee Monologue
(Book, Chatham Press)
by Marshall J. Dodge and Walter Howe,
photographs by Mary Eastman
Text and photography version of the story
told on *Bert and I Stem Inflation.*

How to Talk Yankee, featuring Tim Sample and Robert Bryan
(Album, Bert and I, Inc.)
This album recorded in 1982 was Tim Sample's first for the
"Bert and I" label and pairs him with Robert Bryan to create a
"talking dictionary" of Maine dialectic speech. Words include:
"Ayuh," "Chadge," "Gawmy," and "Scrid."

A Whale's Tale and Other Stories from Down East
(CD, Bert and I, Inc.)
by Marshall Dodge and Robert Bryan
A repacked collection of stories aimed, somewhat, at children.
Notable for including the original "The Bert and I Song" by
Marshall Dodge's brother, Fred.

Bert and I . . . And Other Stories from Down East
(Book, Down East Books)
by Marshall Dodge and Robert Bryan
Illustrated by Mark Andres
Text versions, with illustrations, of some stories from the origi-
nal *Bert and I* album.

Bert and I For Kids All of Ages
(Book, Down East Books)
By Marshall Dodge and Robert Bryan
Illustrated by Edith Heyck
A short three-story collection, with color illustrations, aimed at
children. Features "By a Fluke," "The Pet Turkey," and
"Gagnon."